NATURE ANATOMY NOTEBOOK

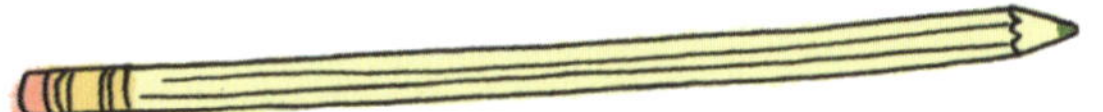

Julia Rothman

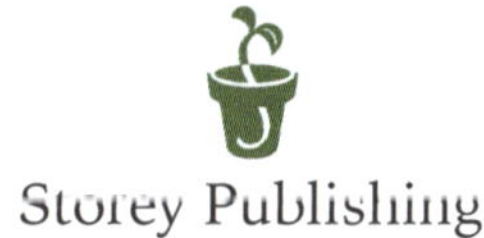

Storey Publishing

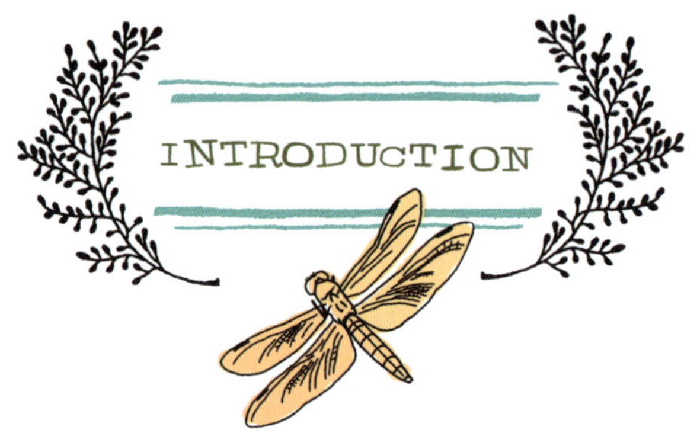

When I'm lying in the grass in Brooklyn's Prospect Park, I like to take a close look at the spot where the roots go into the soil. I try to figure out which trees I'm surrounded by. I watch the clouds shift form above me ever so slowly. I try to be always observing, and I carry a small sketchbook wherever I go.

There are so many moments when we find ourselves waiting. Instead of looking at your phone, you can be surveying and writing and drawing the world around you. This journal is meant to be a guide for just that. It's a place where you can record the plants, flowers, and animals you see. It's a reminder to take a moment to examine their intricate parts, and it's a place to document your findings.

Throughout the pages of this notebook, you'll find some instructional drawings. These will help you understand how to begin to build a form when drawing. I encourage you to sketch directly from nature. Pay attention to the

entire subject as a whole, especially
the silhouette it makes, before
going in to draw the finer details.
Inspect the things in nature you
think you already know: dandelion
petals, the back of a leaf, the
movement of a squirrel, the way a
plant reacts in the wind. I always
find it most exciting when I make a
discovery about something I look at
every day.

Start with pencil sketches and
work your way into ink drawings. I
usually draw with a regular Uniball
pen — there are always a few in
the bottom of my tote bag — and I
work fast. You can also use colored
pencils or pastels to lend your

drawing some delicate color. When
I paint, I use gouache. I like the
flat, bright color. Another option is
watercolor. With watercolor, you
can paint layers to create depth
and shadow.

It has been so wonderful to see
your responses to *Farm Anatomy*,
Nature Anatomy, and *Food
Anatomy*. Thank you for sharing
so many pictures of yourselves and
your kids learning and drawing from
the books. I cherish each of the
photos and it encourages me to
create more! I hope you will continue
to share these moments, and also
share what you observe and draw
in this notebook so I can see!

xo *Julia Rothman*

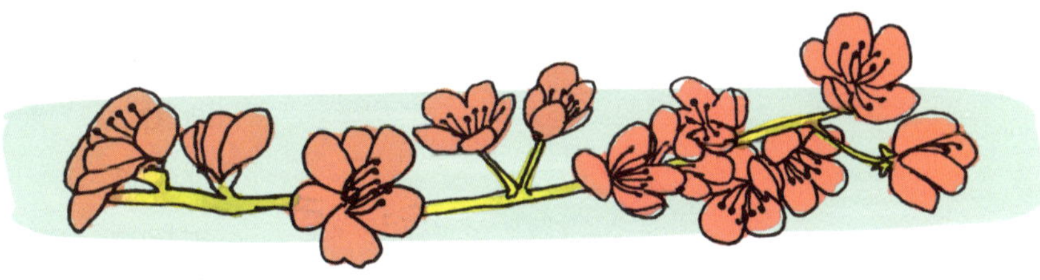

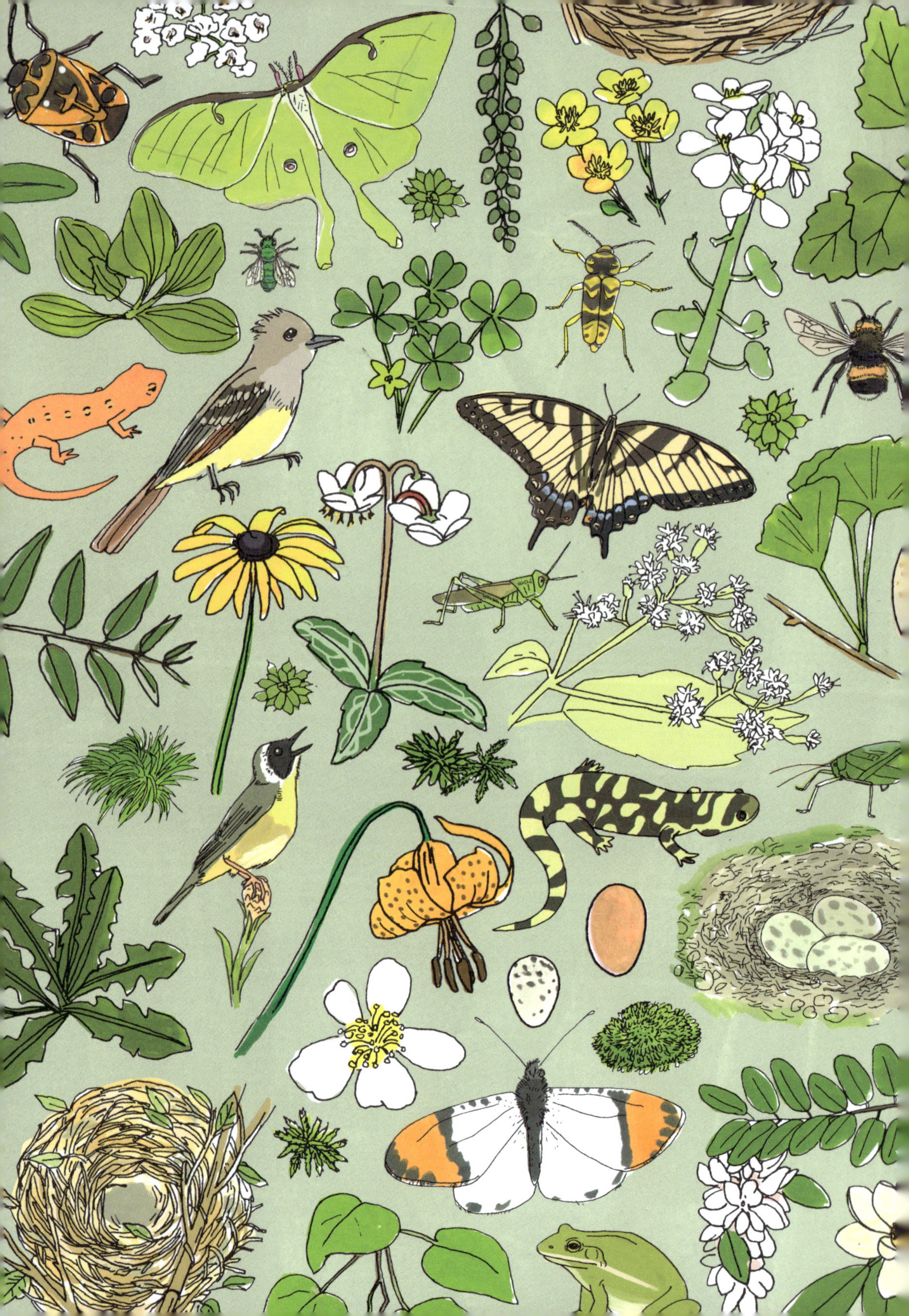

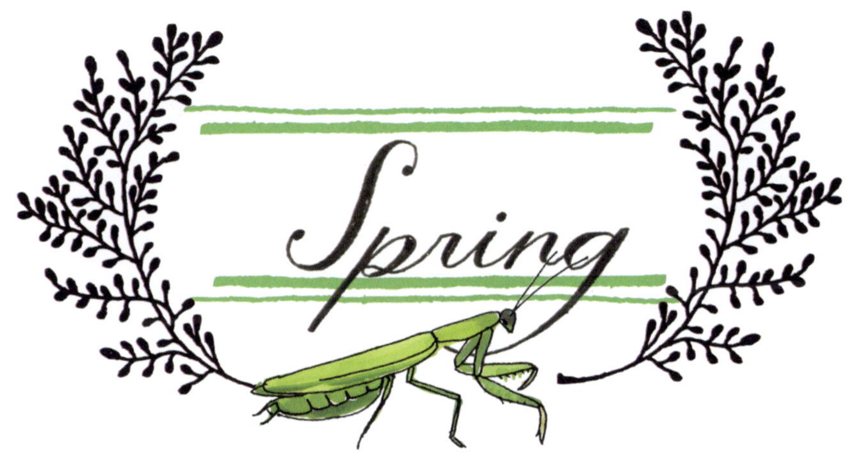
Spring

YEAR
MONTH

YEAR
MONTH

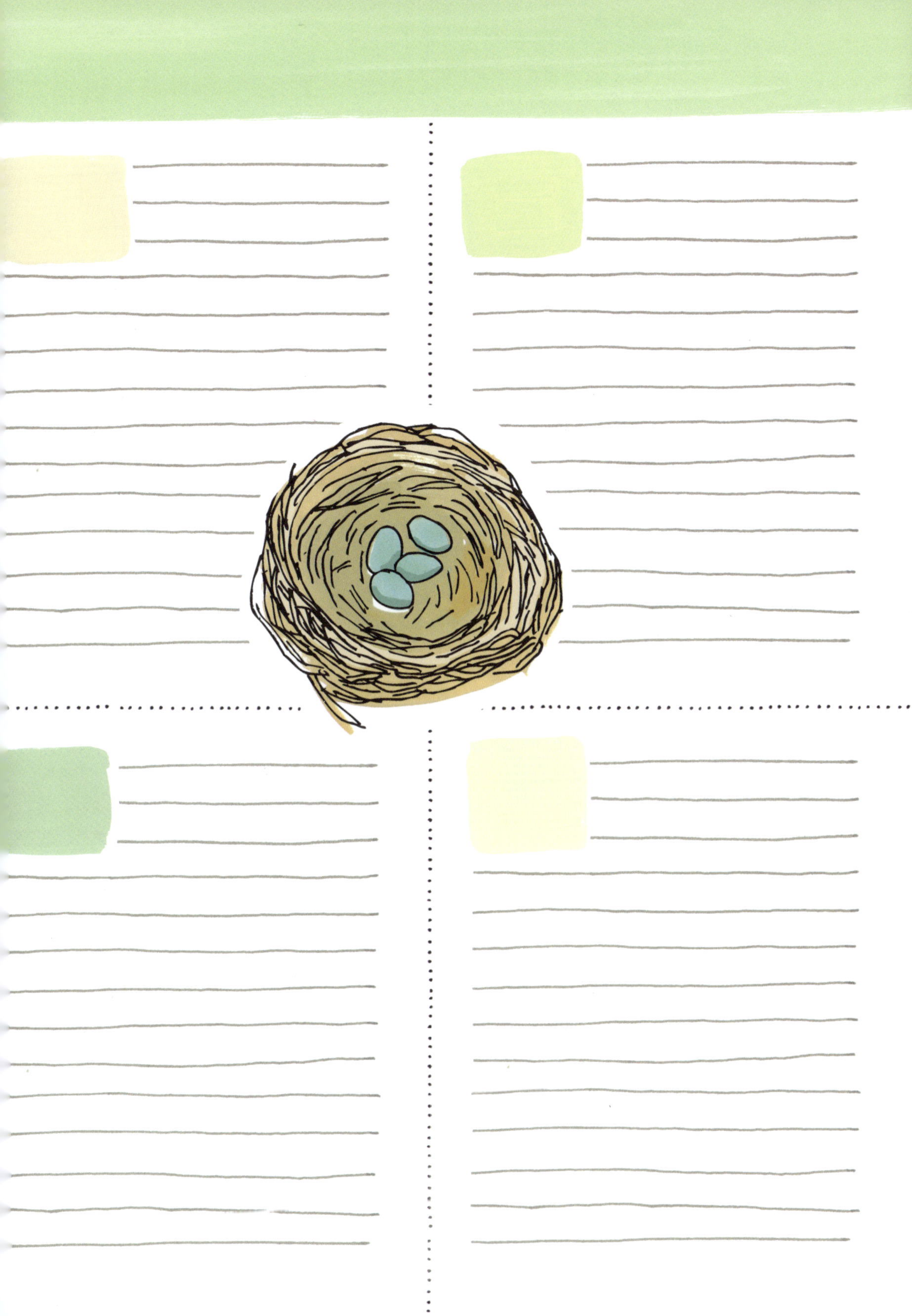

YEAR
MONTH

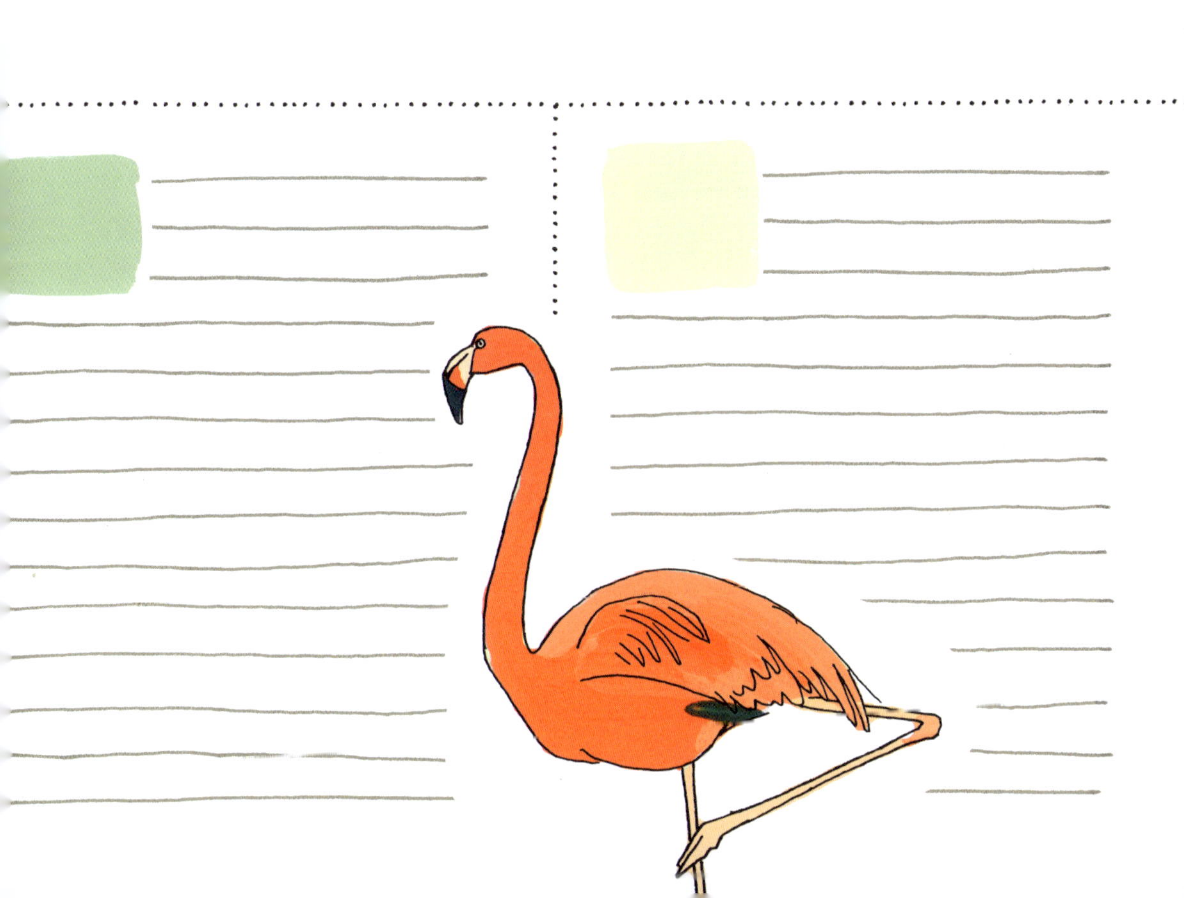

YEAR   MONTH

HOW TO DRAW A FROG

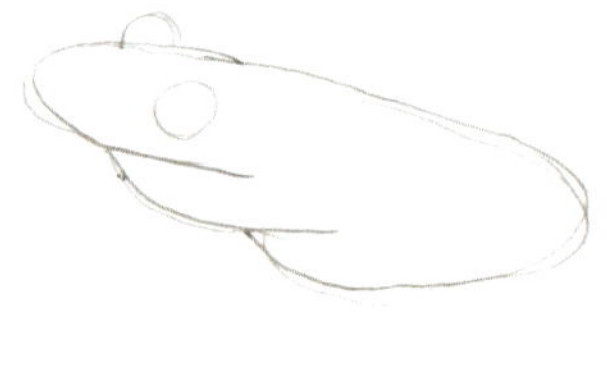

In pencil, sketch the basic outline of the body and the eyeballs.

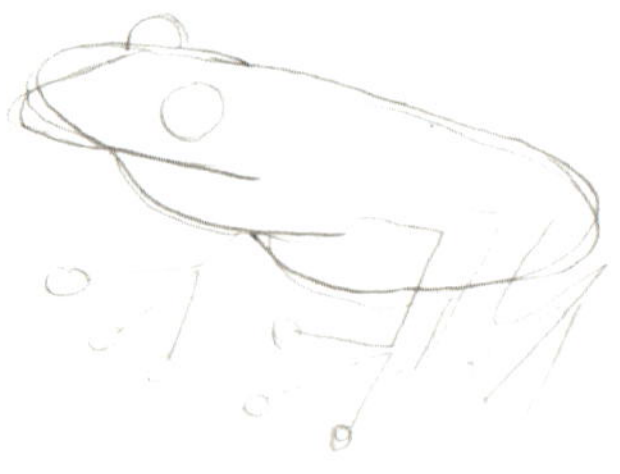

Sketch in the outline of the legs and feet.

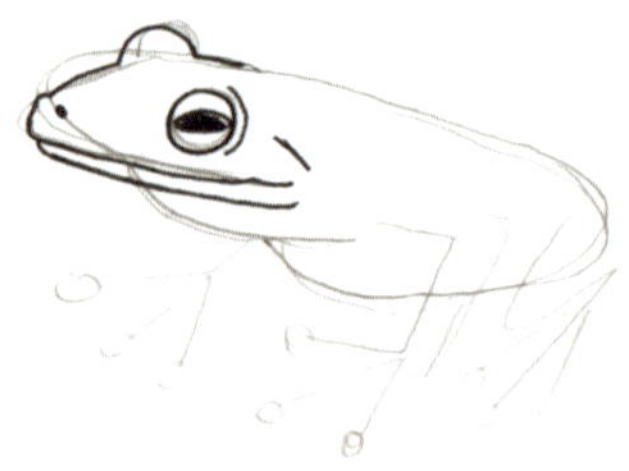

Ink the head. Add a pupil and a nostril.

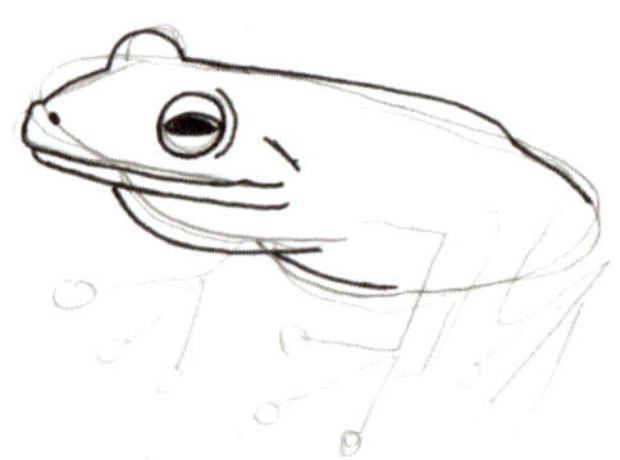

Ink the rest of the body, tracing over the pencil outline with pen. Don't forget his throat.

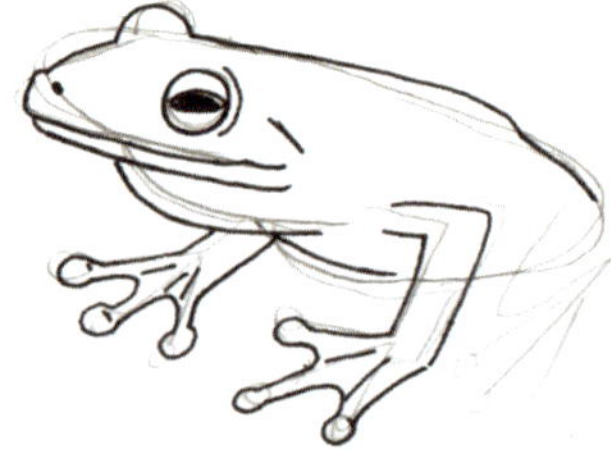

Ink in the front legs and webbed feet.

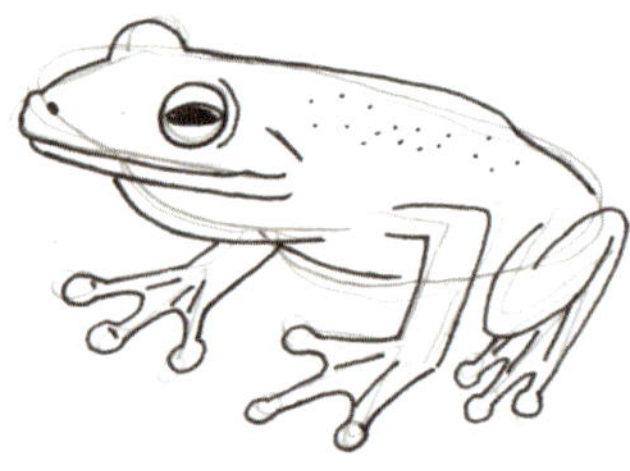

Finish with the hind leg. Add dots across his back for skin detail.

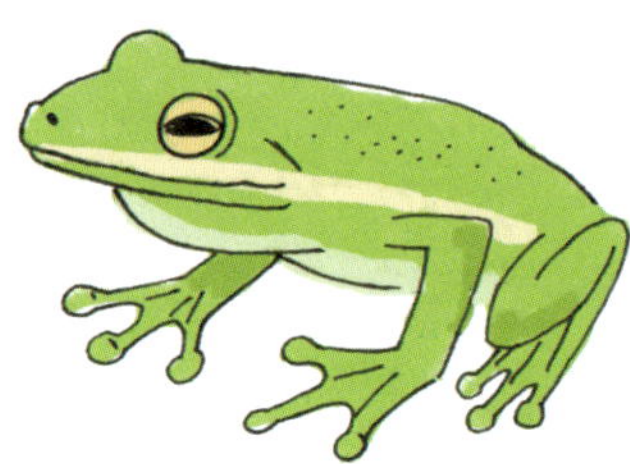

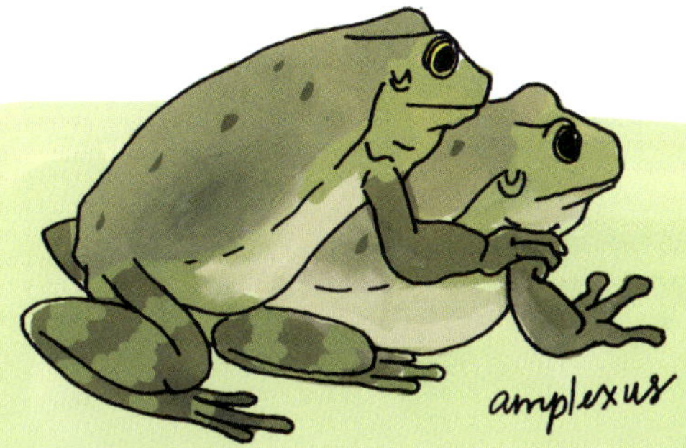

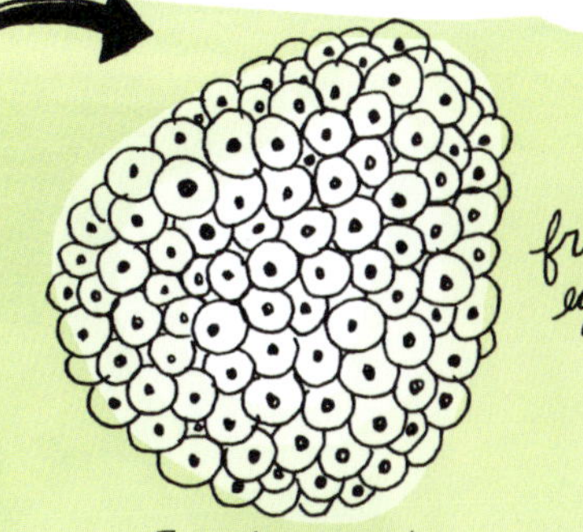

Following loud and elaborate courtship displays in the spring, frogs mate in the water in an embrace called amplexus that may last several days.

Female frogs lay sticky clusters of eggs in calm water.

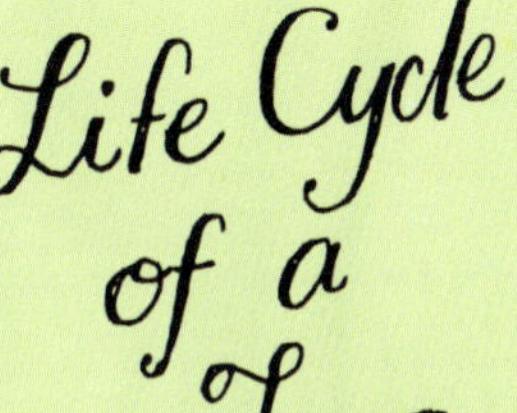

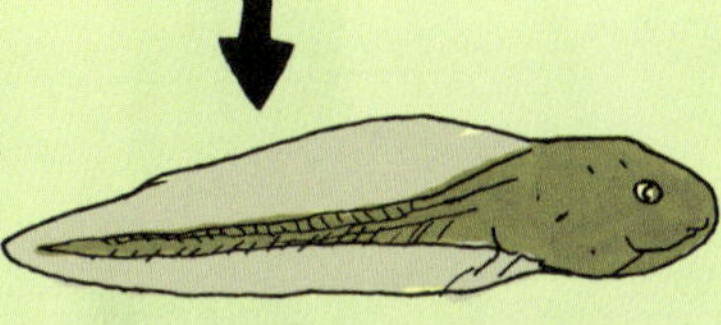

Tadpoles emerge after a week or two.

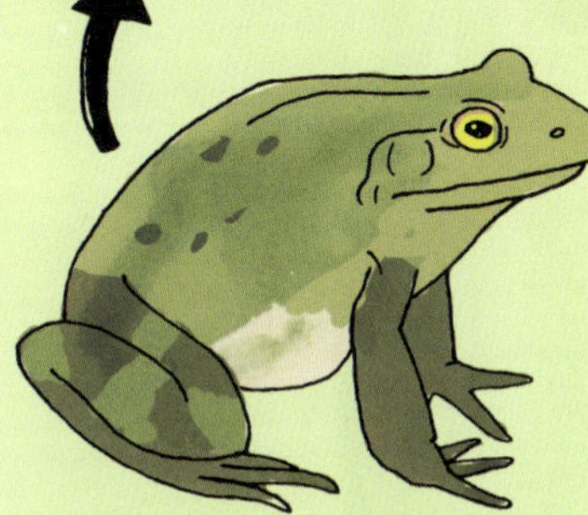

At 12 weeks, froglets have absorbed all but a stub of their tails.

Tadpoles have rudimentary gills. They may stick themselves to plants until they are strong enough to swim and begin eating algae.

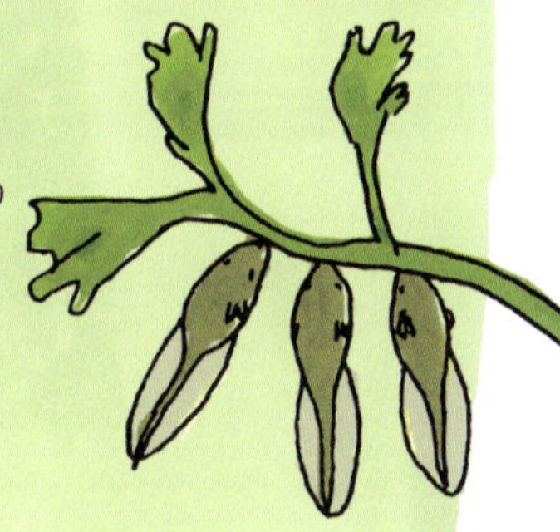

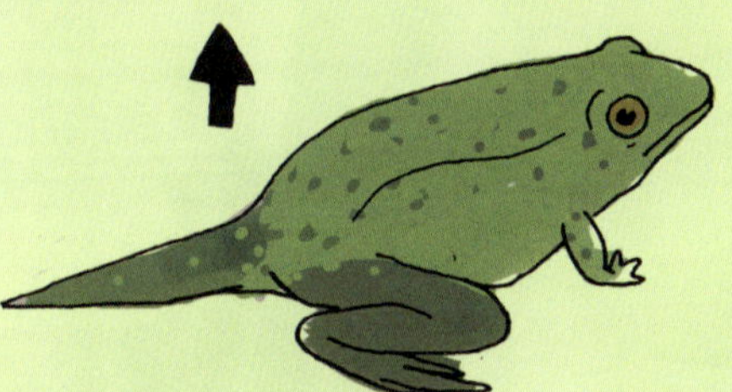

By 9 weeks old, they look like tiny frogs with long tails.

From 6 to 9 weeks after hatching, arms and legs grow elbows-first from the tadpole's sides.

YEAR
MONTH

YEAR   MONTH

YEAR
MONTH

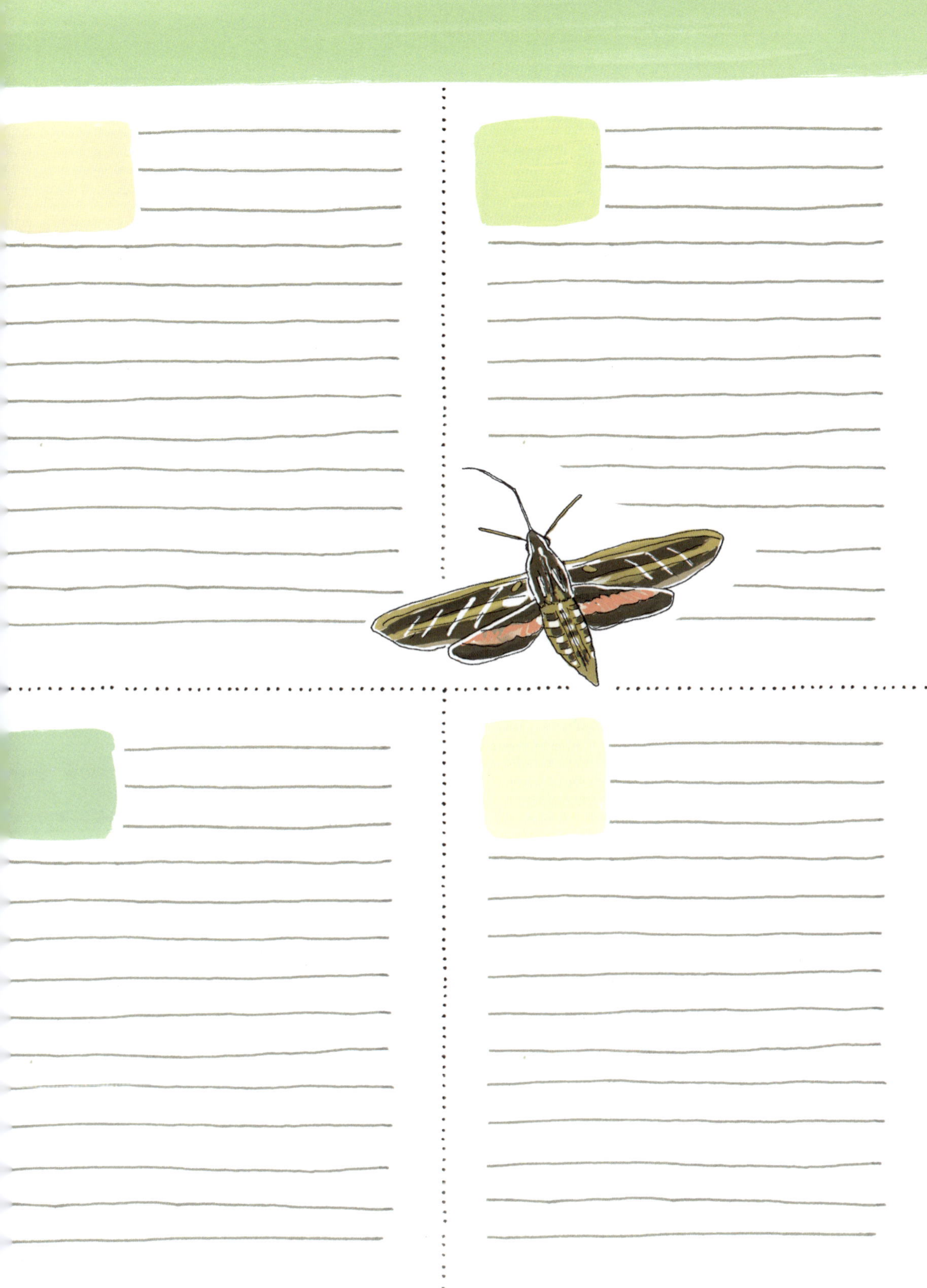

YEAR
MONTH

HOW TO DRAW A FERN

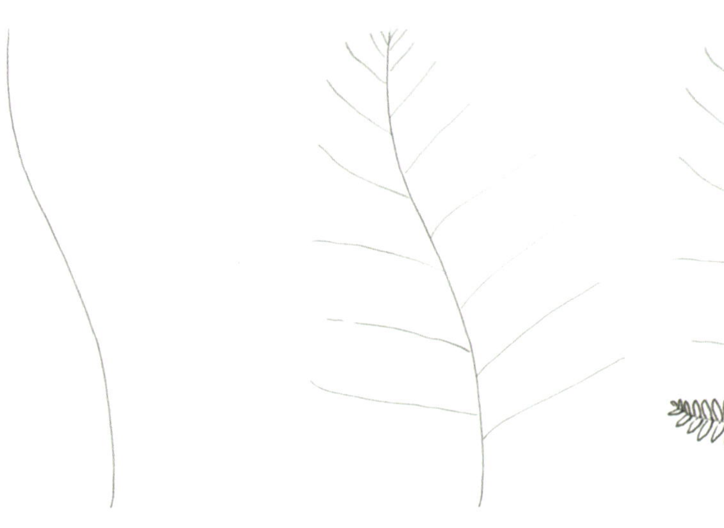

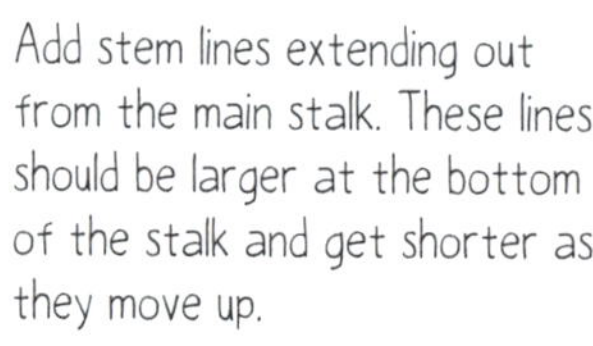

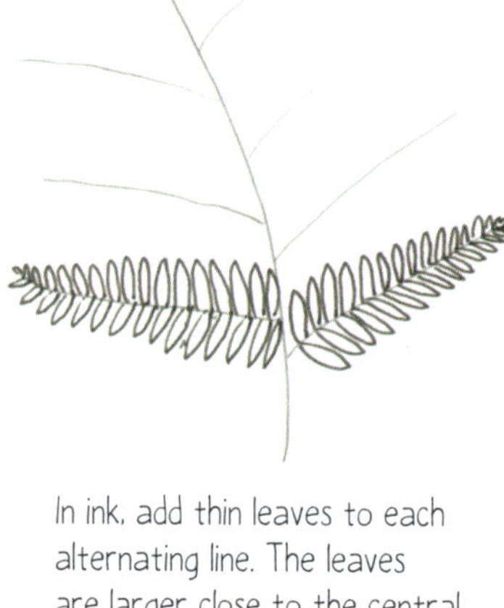

In pencil, draw one waving line that will be the central stalk.

Add stem lines extending out from the main stalk. These lines should be larger at the bottom of the stalk and get shorter as they move up.

In ink, add thin leaves to each alternating line. The leaves are larger close to the central stalk and get smaller as they move out to the tip.

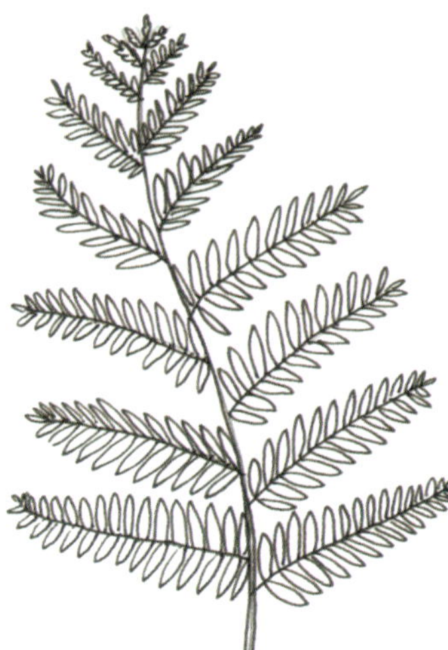

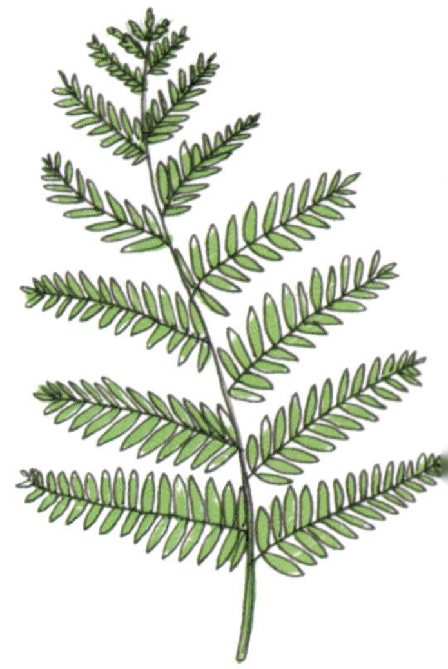

The leaves also get smaller as they move up the central stalk toward the top.

When the leaves are finished, use ink to carefully trace over the pencil lines of the central stalk and the alternating lines extending out from the stalk.

Add color. Ferns can be varying shades of green or brown.

ANATOMY OF A FERN

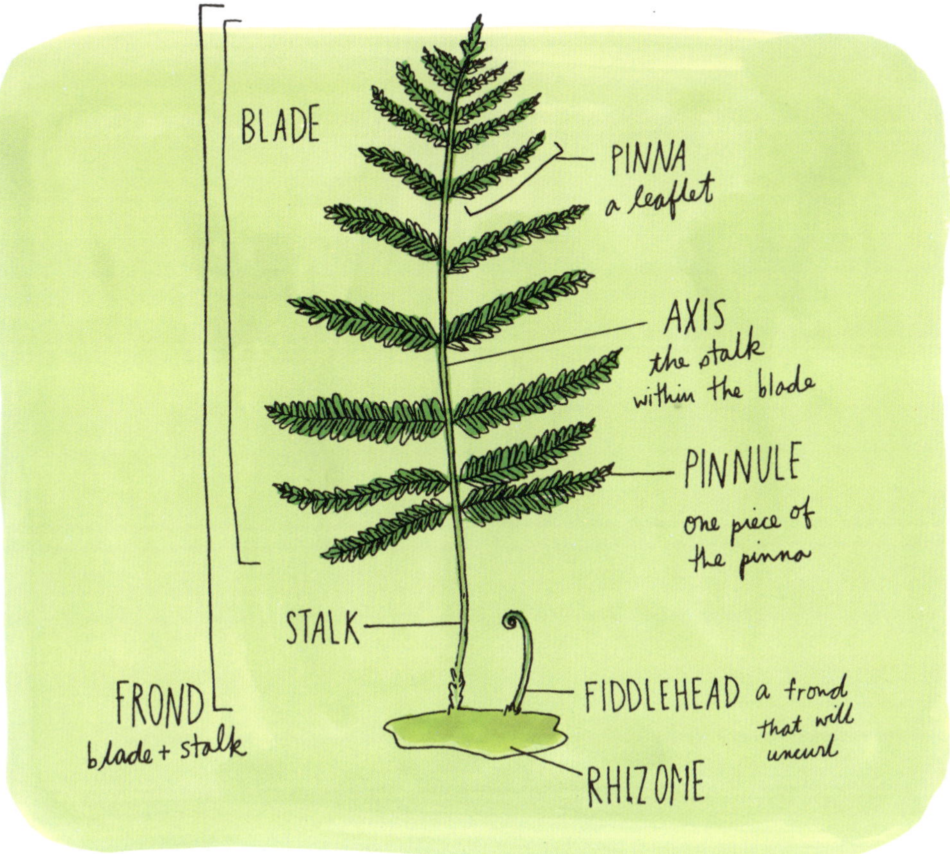

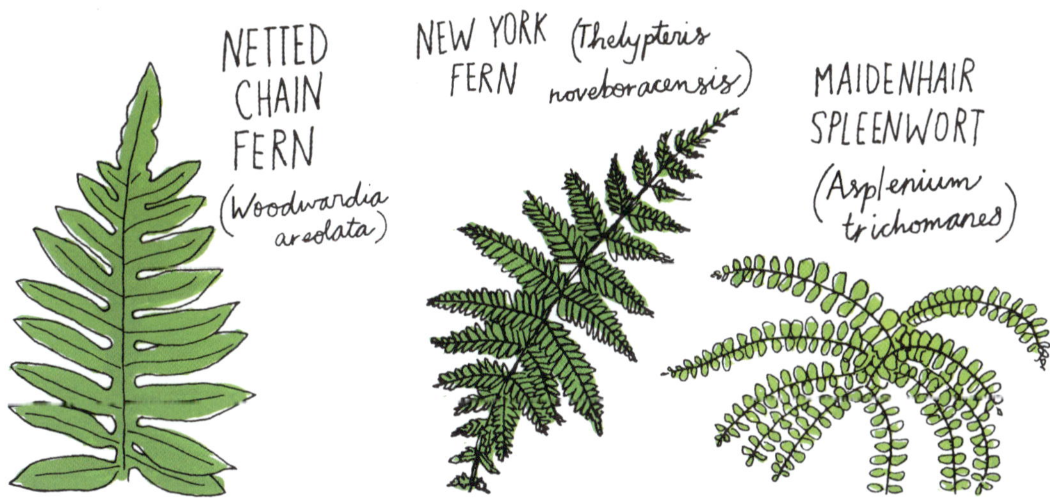

YEAR   MONTH

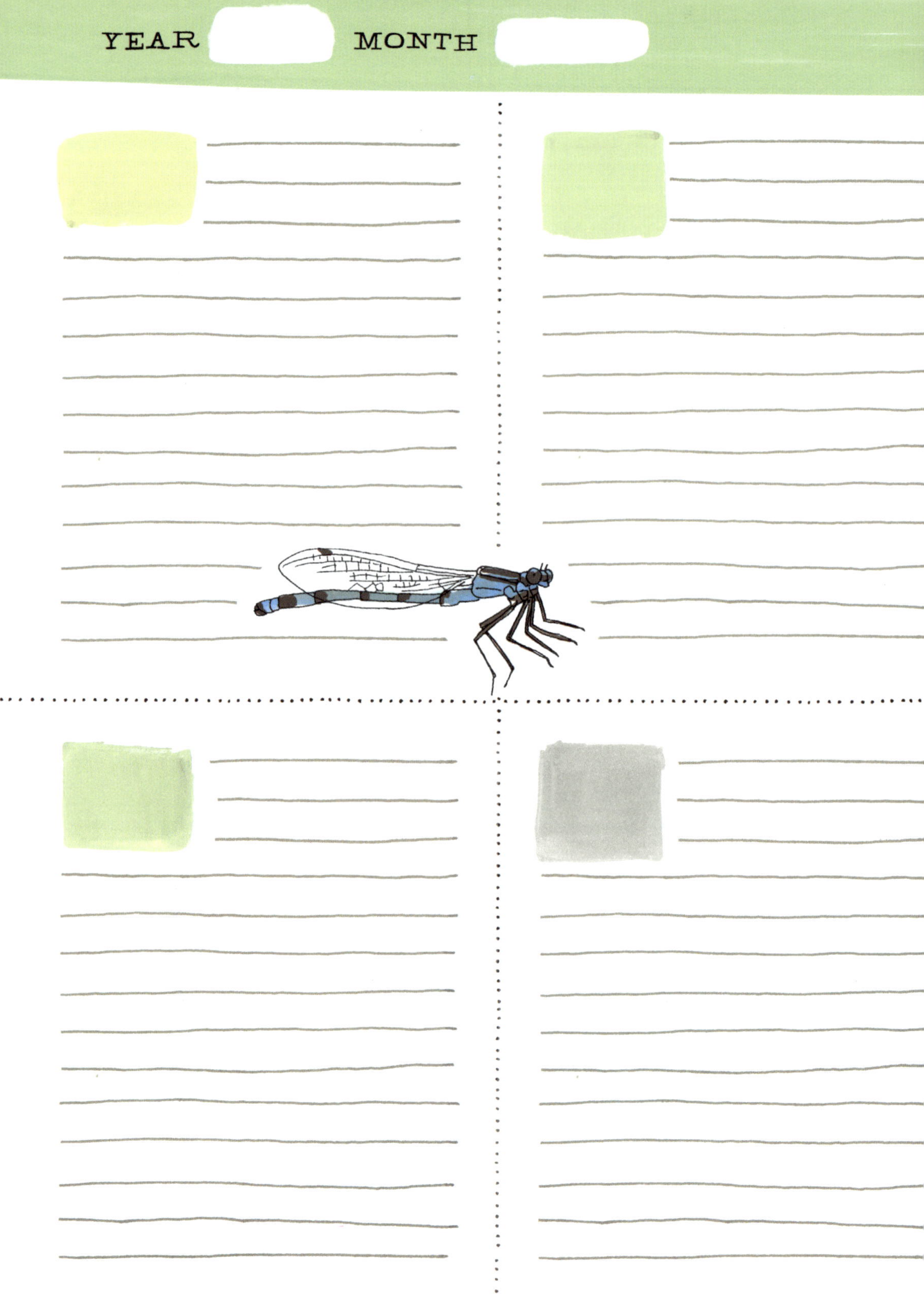

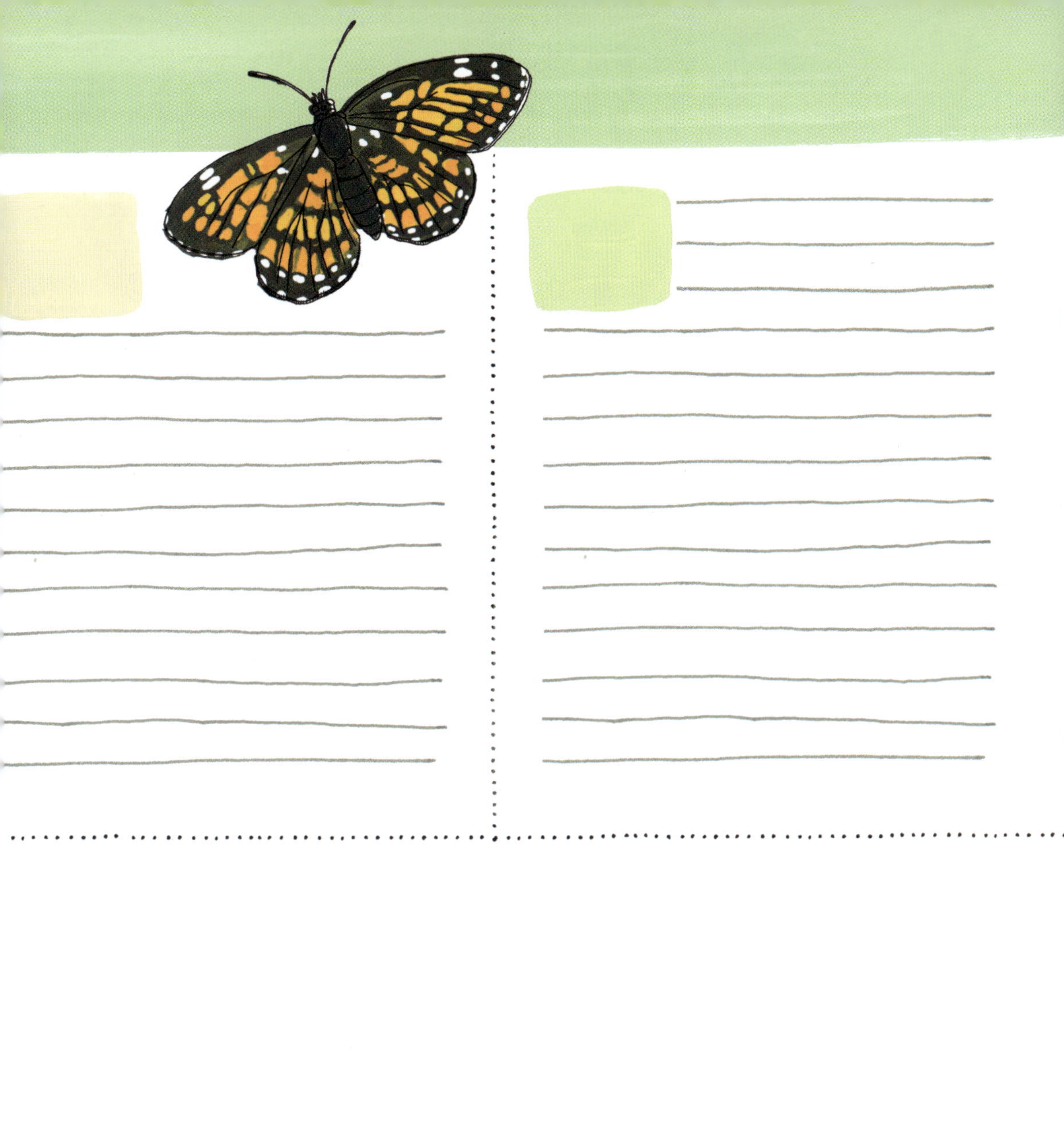

YEAR   MONTH

YEAR
MONTH

YEAR
MONTH

YEAR
MONTH

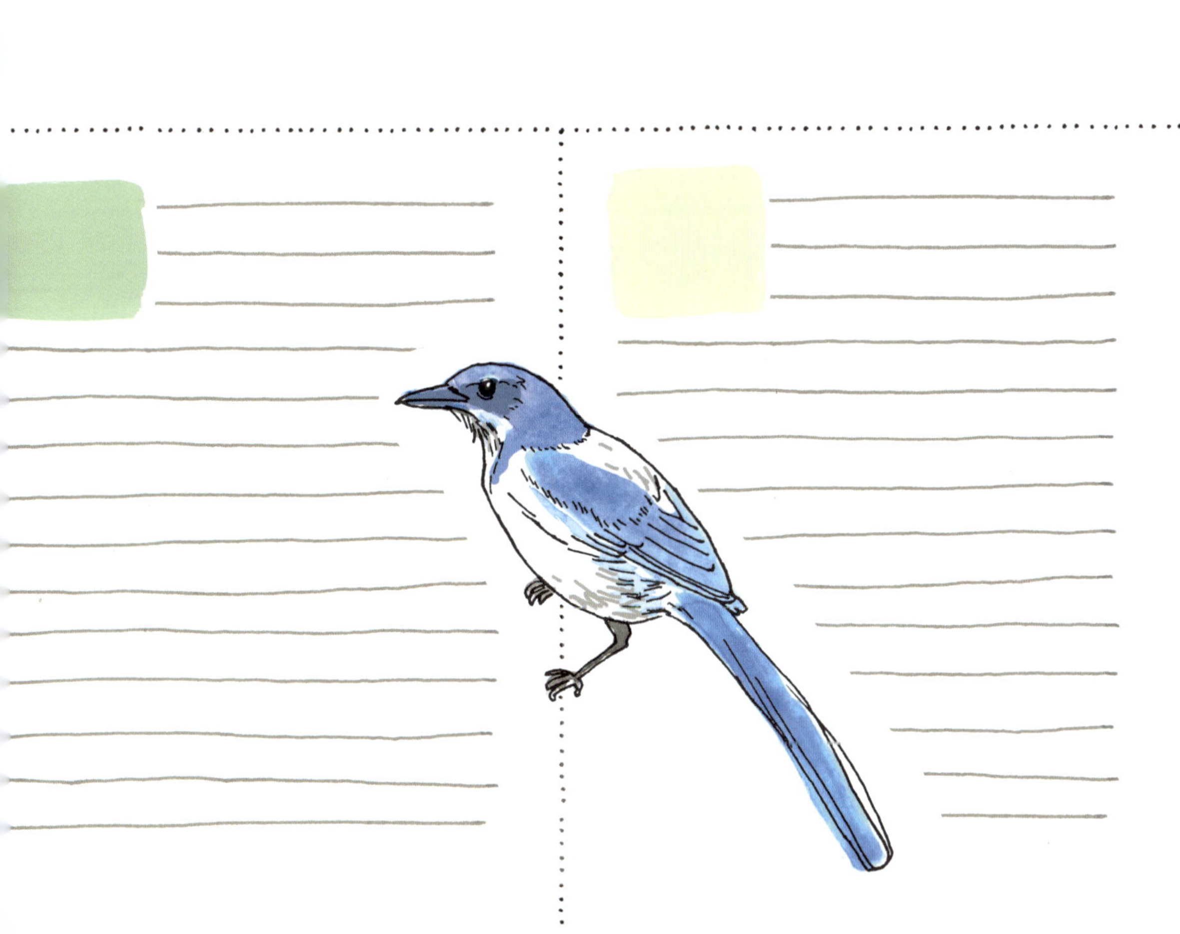

HOW TO DRAW A BIRD

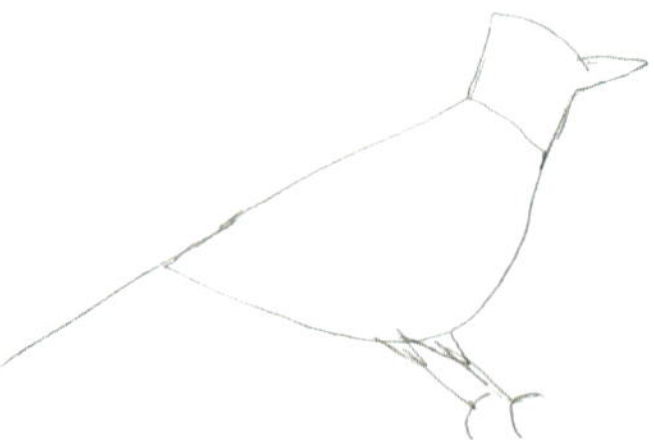

In pencil, sketch the outline of the bird's silhouette.

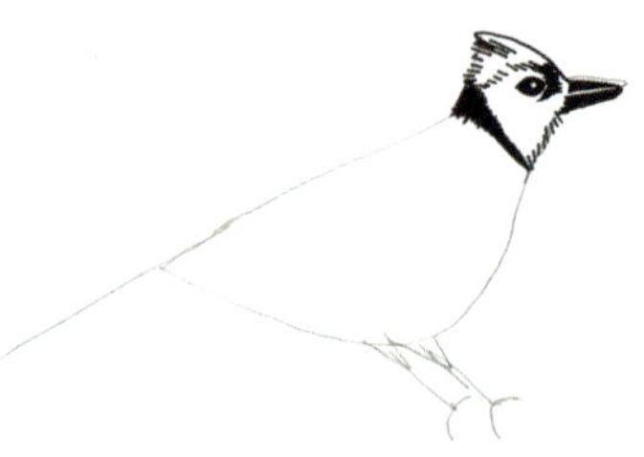

Begin inking the head, eye, and beak.

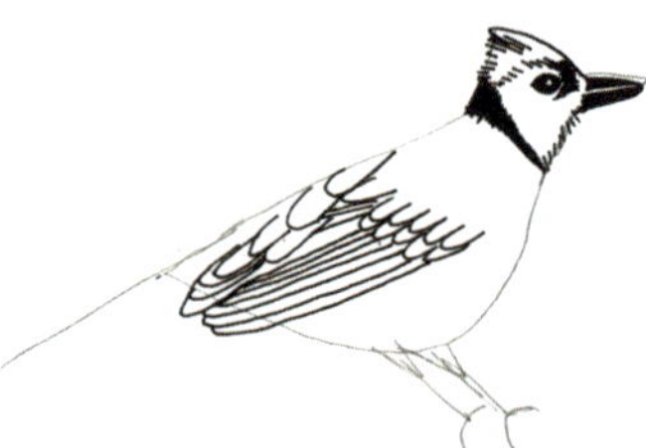

Now ink in the wings. Notice the varying feather sizes and shapes.

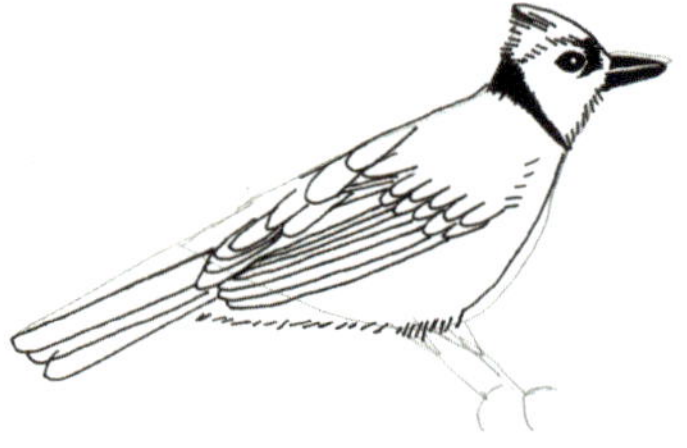

Ink the tail feathers and the underbelly of the bird, called the flank. Complete the outline of the body in ink.

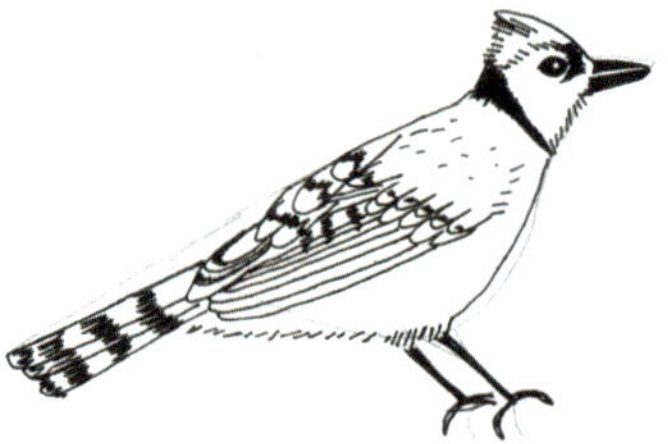

Add some detail markings to the wings, and ink the legs and feet.

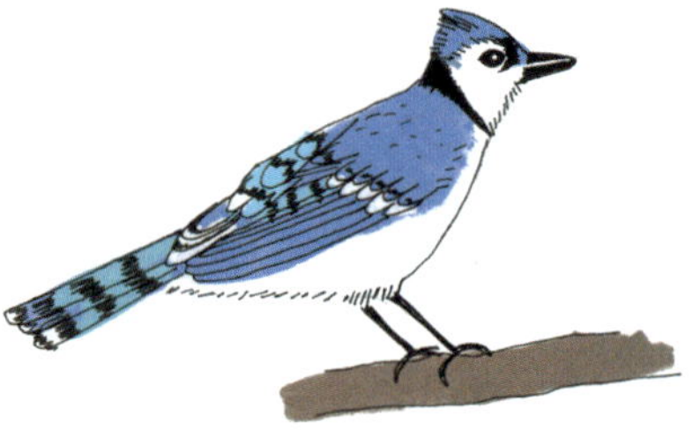

You can add a perch for her to stand on and some color.

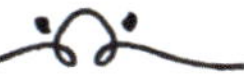

ANATOMY OF A BIRD

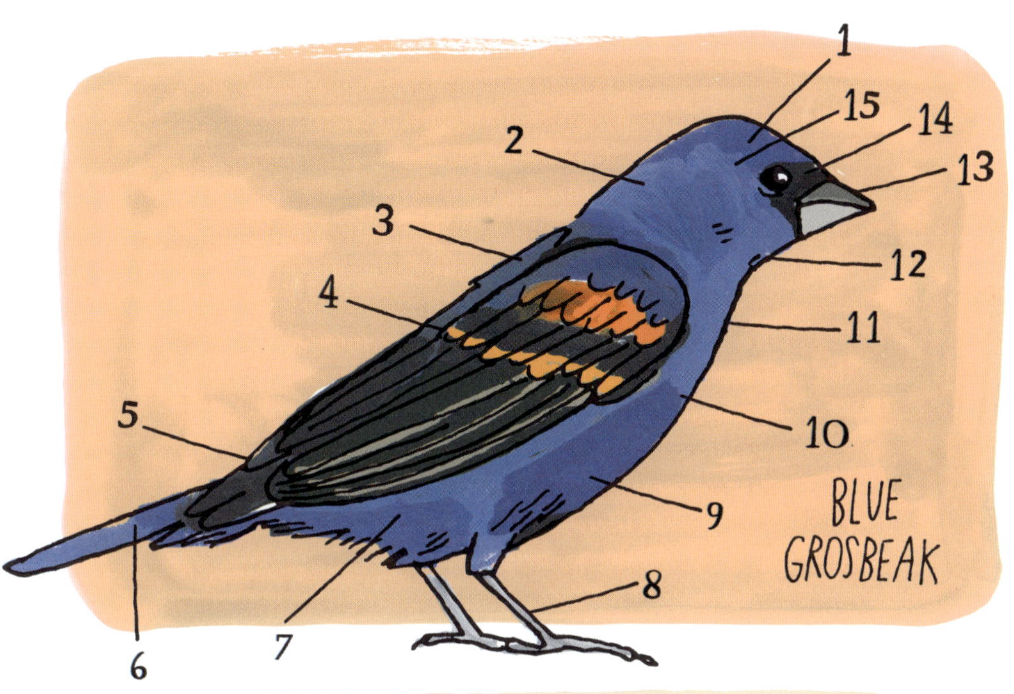

1. crown
2. nape
3. back
4. wing bar
5. rump
6. tail
7. flank
8. tarsus
9. side
10. breast
11. throat
12. chin
13. bill
14. **lore** (area between eye and bill)
15. ear patch

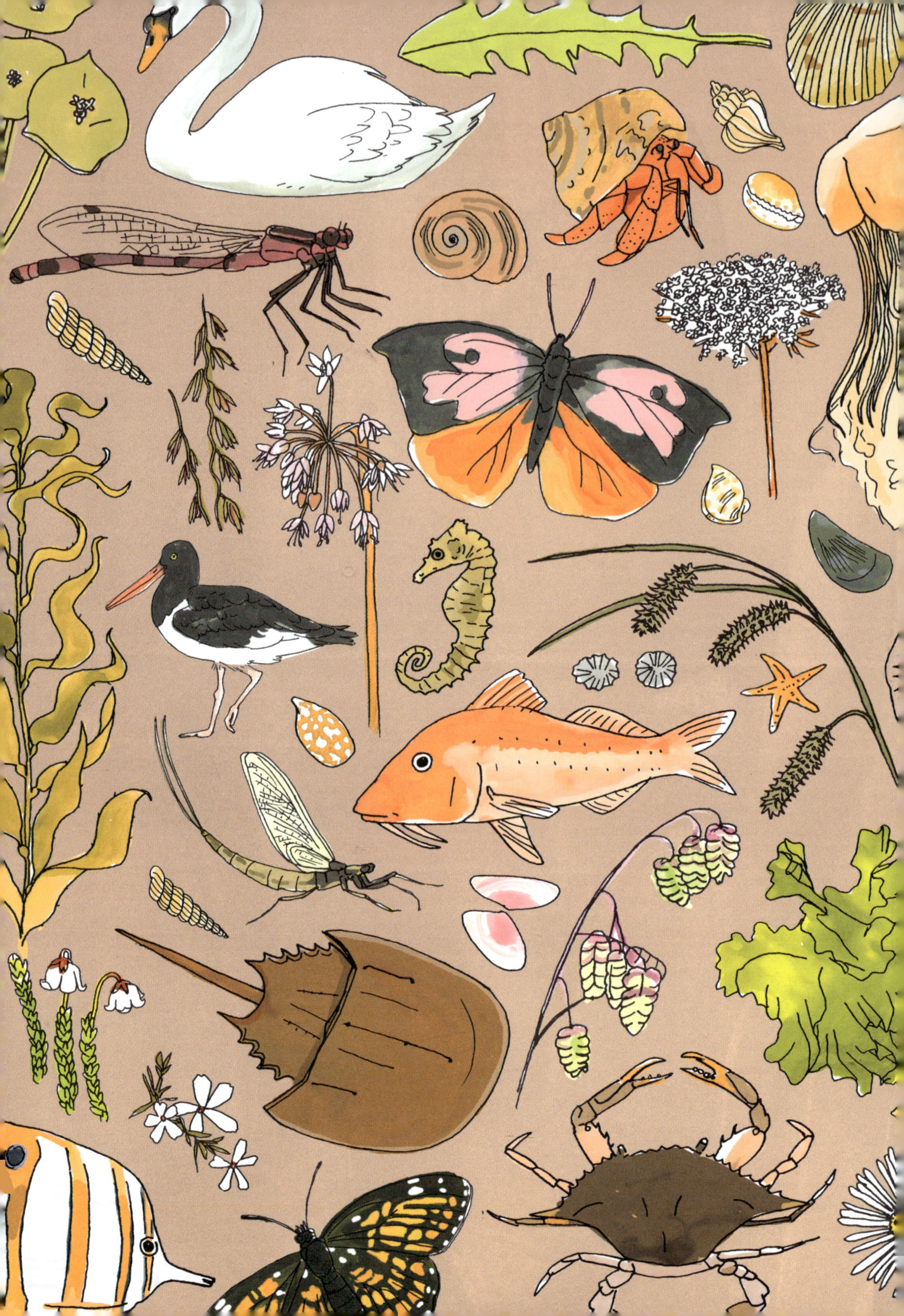

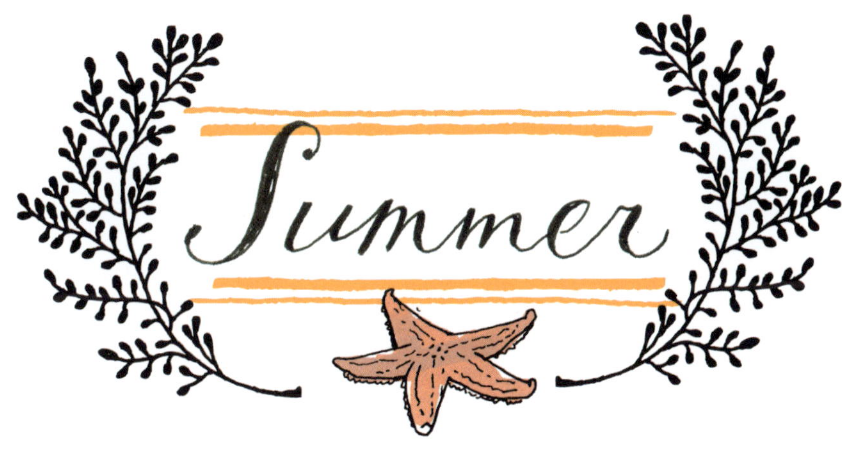

Summer

YEAR
MONTH

YEAR
MONTH

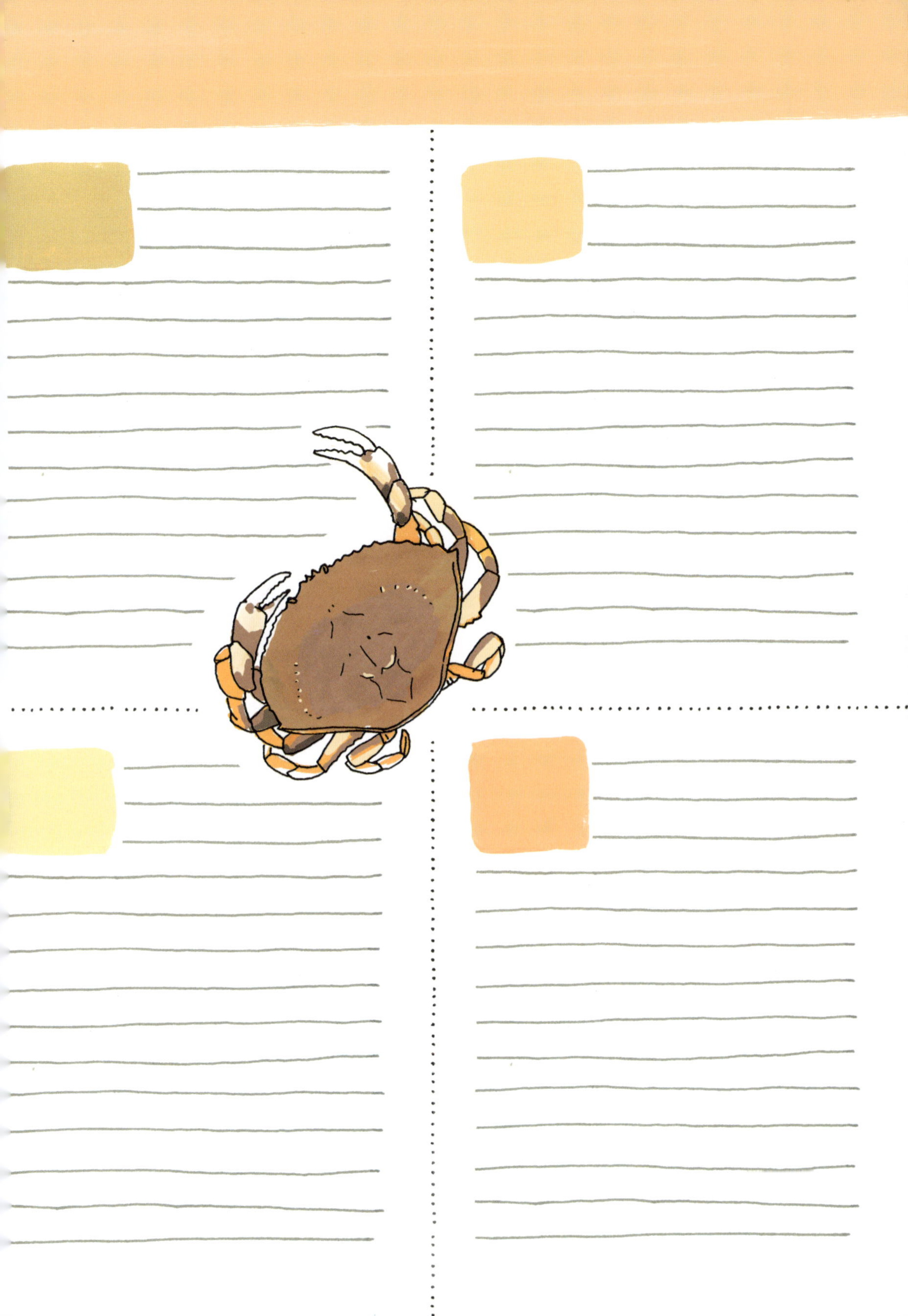

YEAR
MONTH

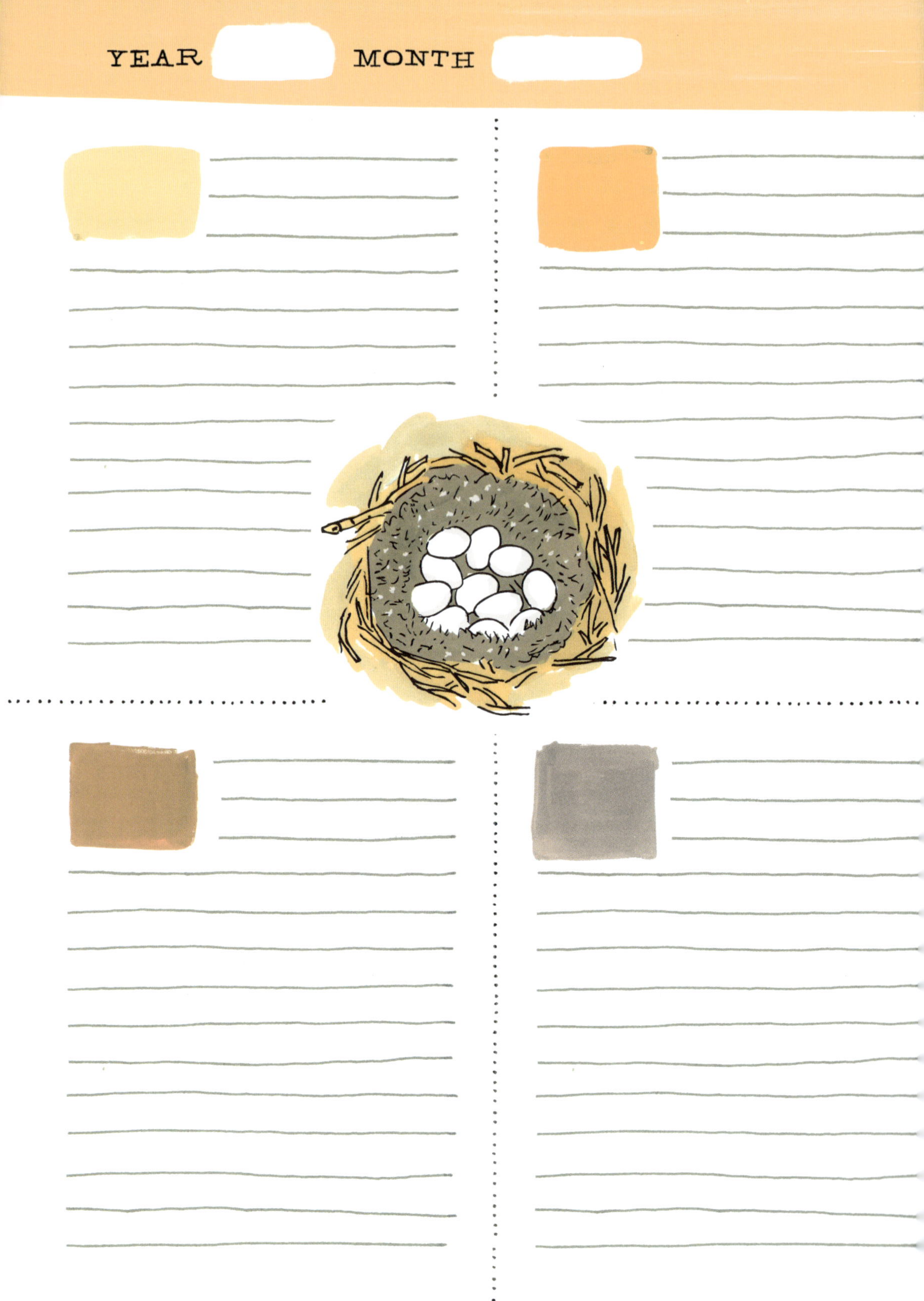

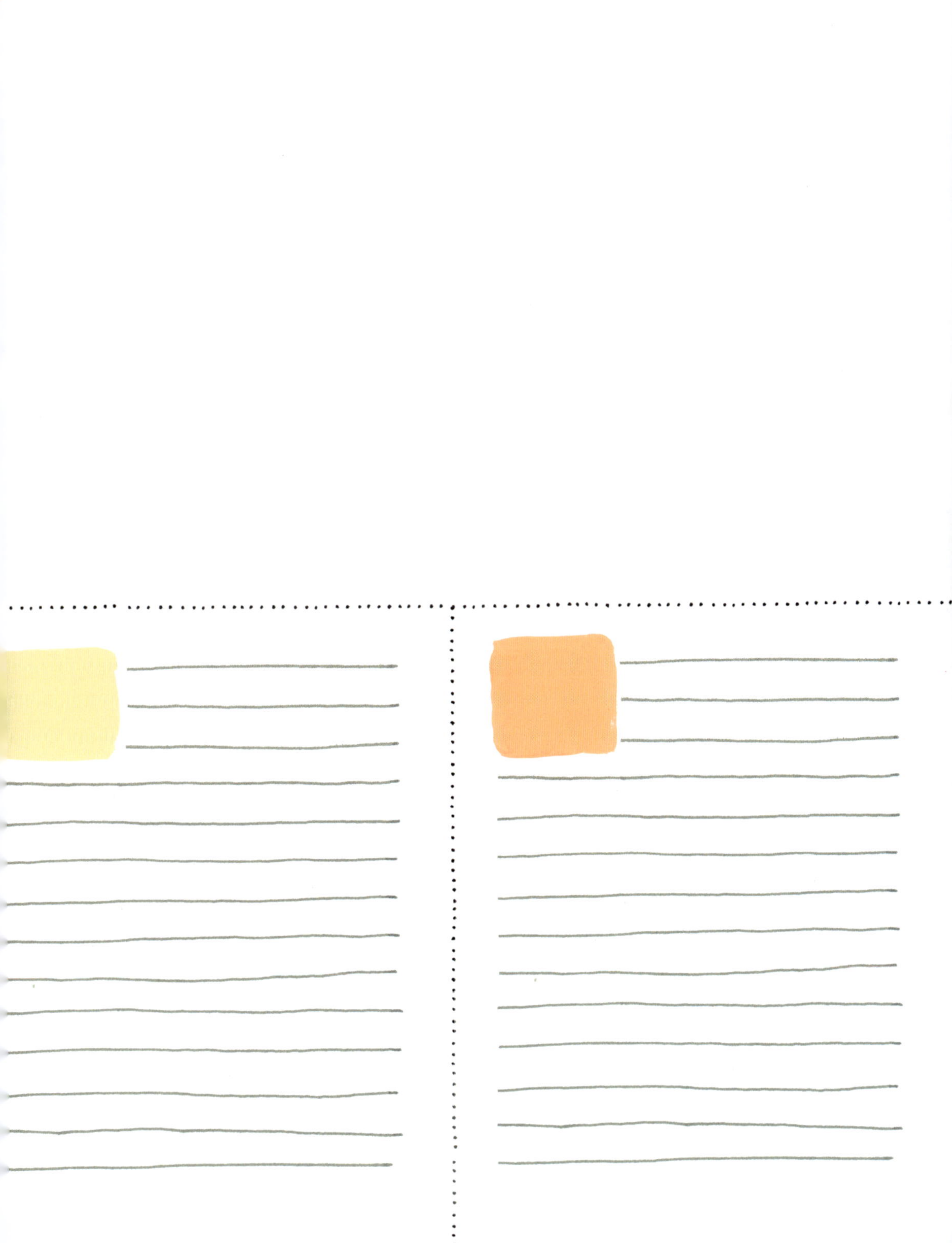

YEAR
MONTH

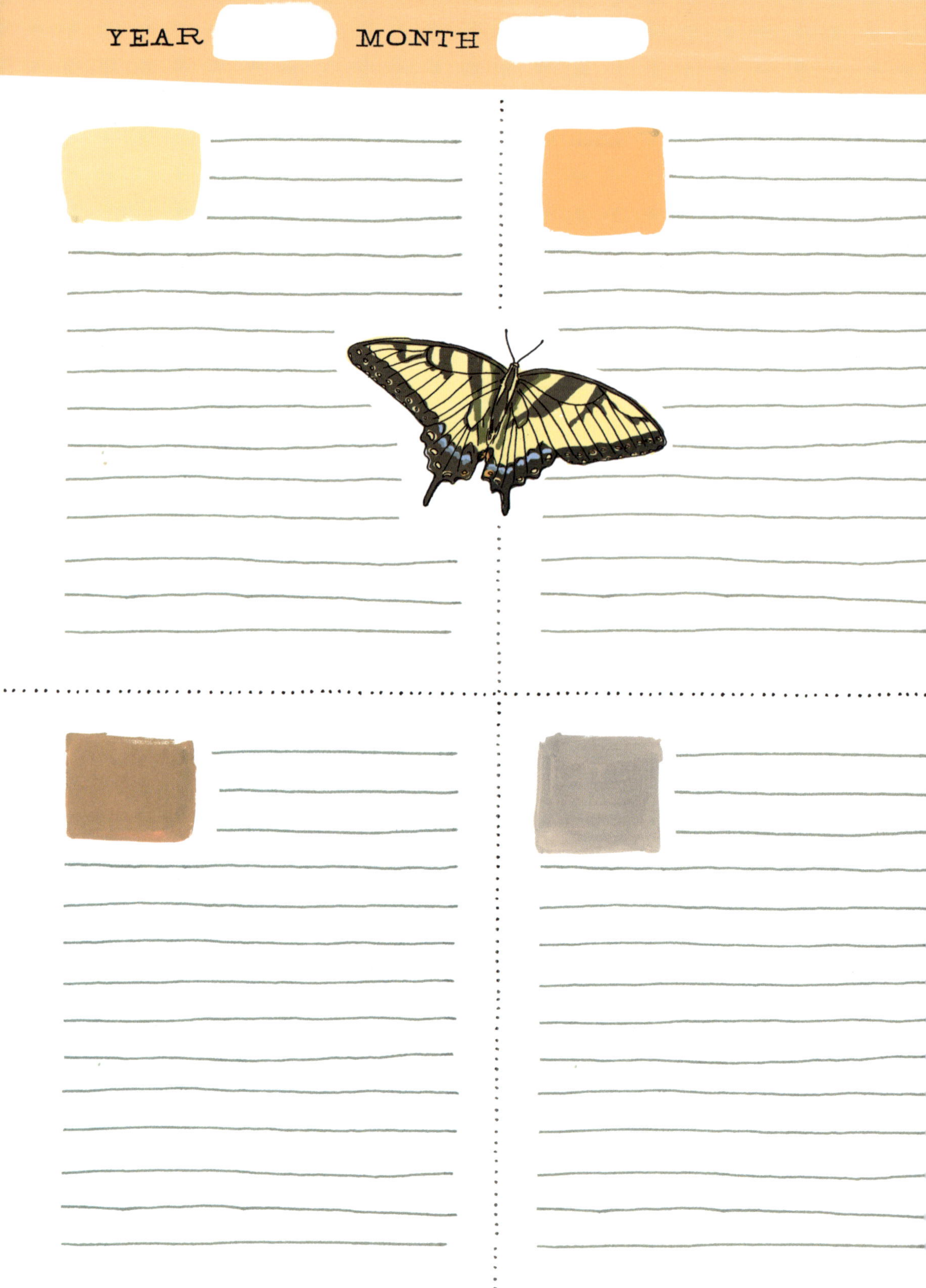

HOW TO DRAW A BUTTERFLY

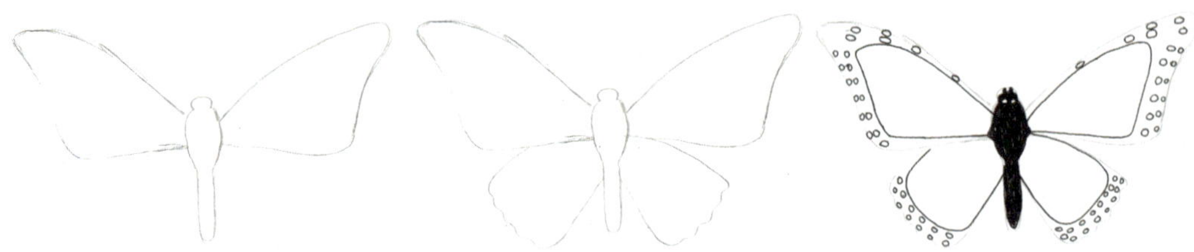

In pencil, sketch the outline of the abdomen and forewings. Try to make the wings as symmetrical as possible.

Sketch in the hindwings, which have bumpy lower edges.

In ink, color in the abdomen. Draw small pairs of circles along the outer edges of the wings. Also draw a line in the interior of each wing that mimics the wing outline.

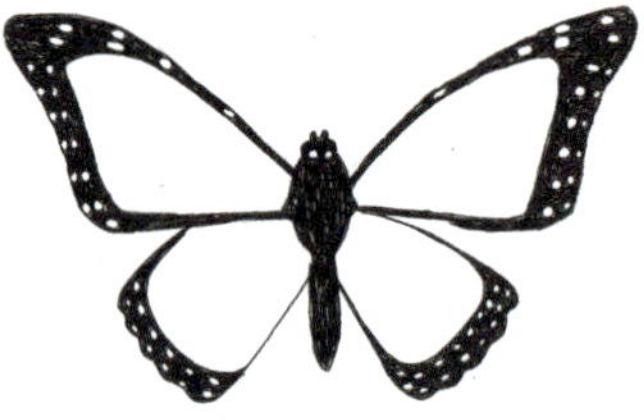

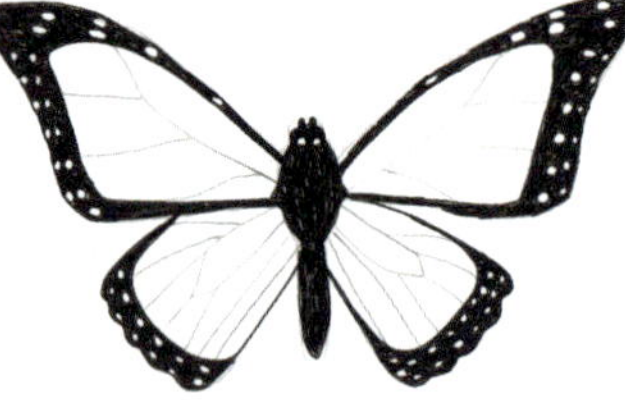

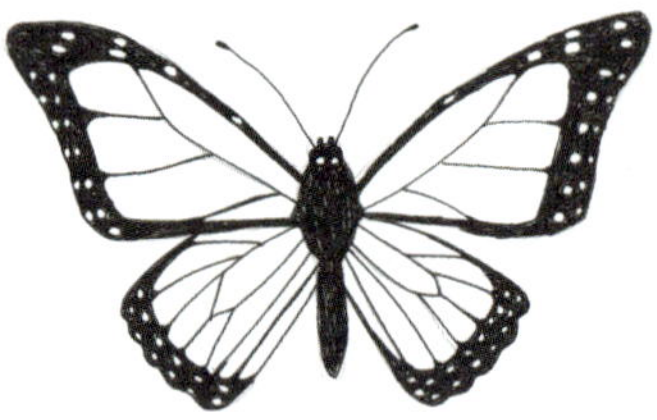

Fill in with ink from the interior line to the exterior pencil outline, but do not fill in the circles.

In pencil, sketch in the wing veins.

Now go over the wing veins in ink. Where the veins touch the interior line, round out the corners and fill them in a little darker. Finish by inking in antennae.

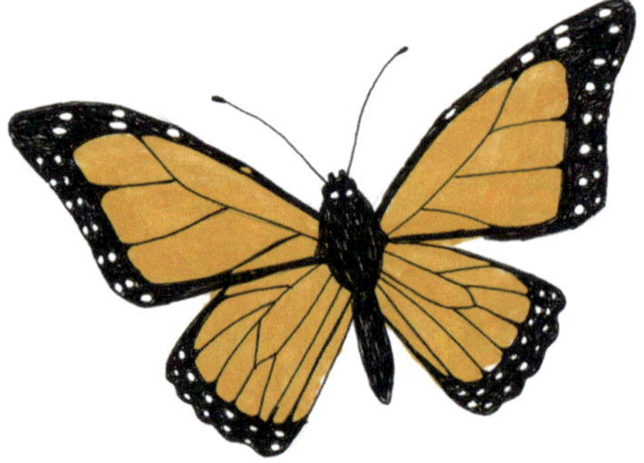

ANATOMY OF A BUTTERFLY

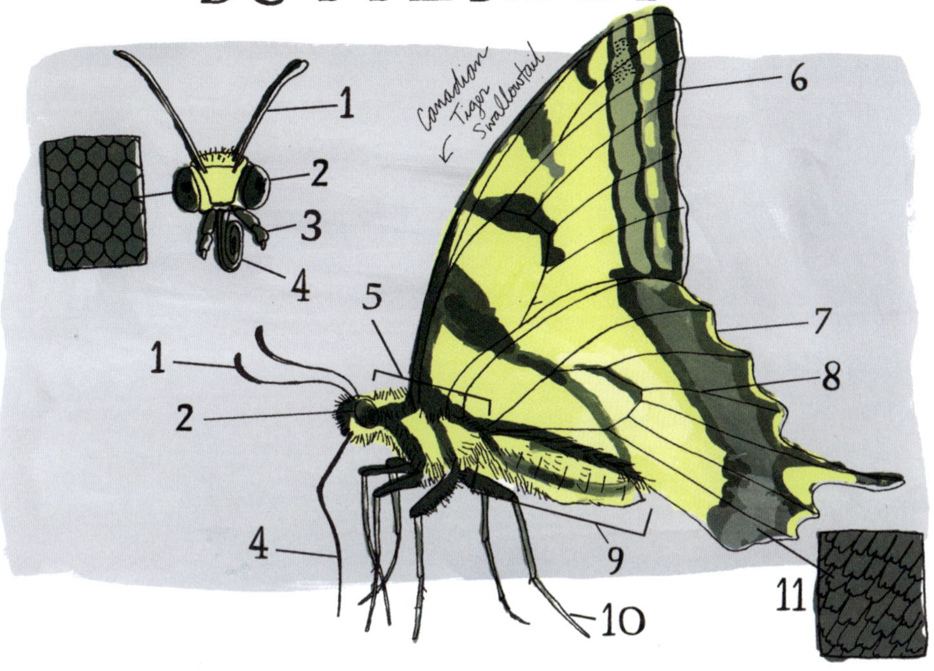

1. **antenna** - used as a form of radar and pheromone detection
2. **compound eye** - has up to 1,700 individual ommatidia (light receptors and lenses)
3. **palpus** - shields the eye from dust; covered in scent-detecting sensors
4. **proboscis** - like a long straw for feeding and drinking
5. **thorax** - three body segments that contain the flight muscles
6. **forewing**
7. **hindwing** — two pairs of overlapping wings that flap and sometimes glide
8. **wing veins** - vary between each genus of butterfly; used in classification
9. **abdomen** - contains the digestive system, respiratory equipment, heart, and sex organs
10. **legs** - butterflies have three pairs
11. **scales** - wings are covered in tiny dustlike colored scales

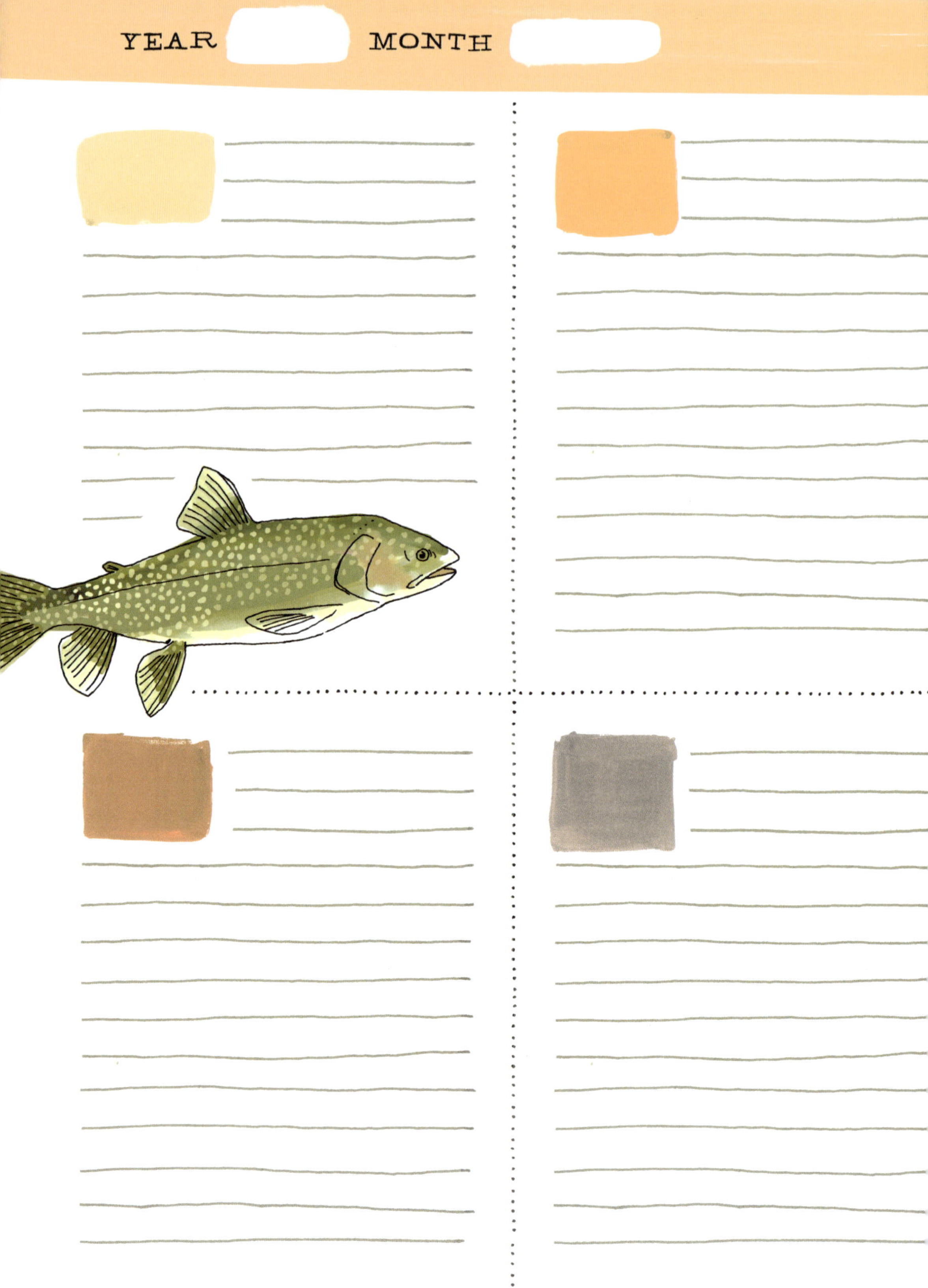

YEAR
MONTH

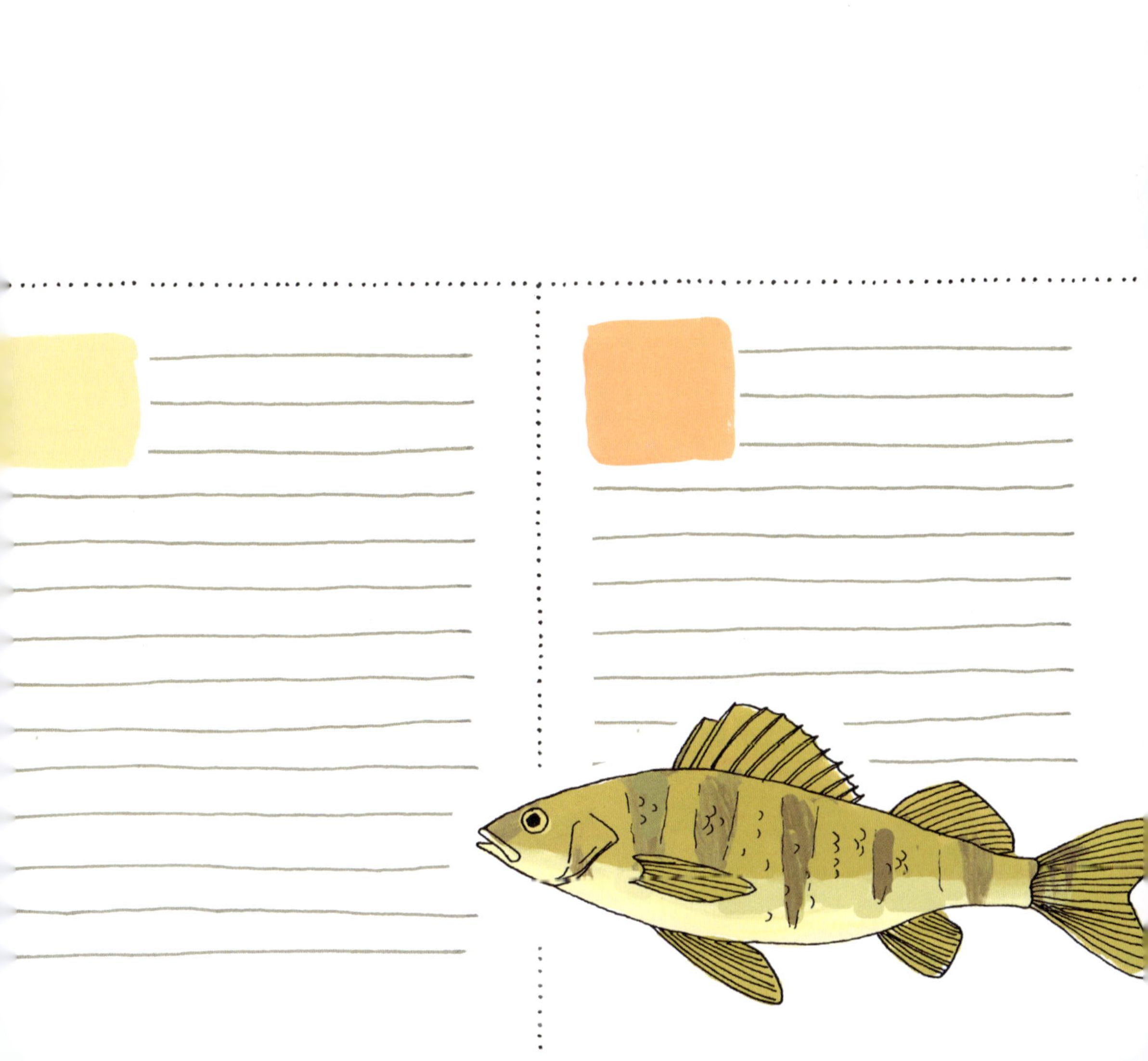

YEAR   MONTH

YEAR
MONTH

YEAR
MONTH

HOW TO DRAW A BEE

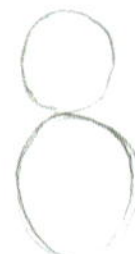 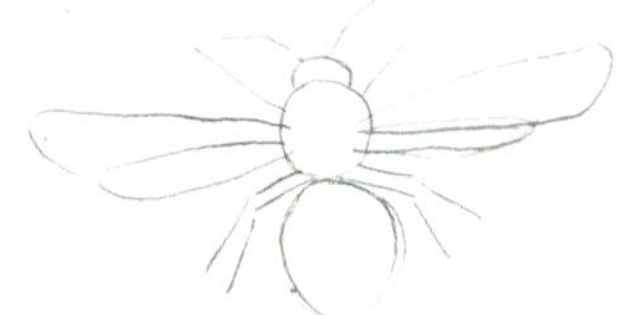 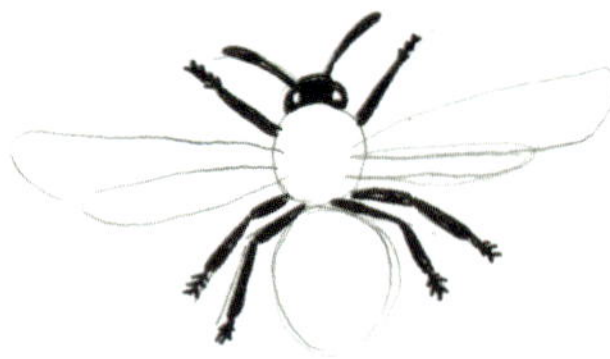

In pencil, sketch two circles for the body. The circle on top, the thorax, should be slightly smaller. The bottom circle, the abdomen, should be slightly larger and elongated.

Sketch in the long forewings, shorter hindwings, and legs. Add a head and antennae.

In ink, fill in the head, leaving two circles for eyes. Fill in the antennae. Fill in the legs and add small claws at the tips.

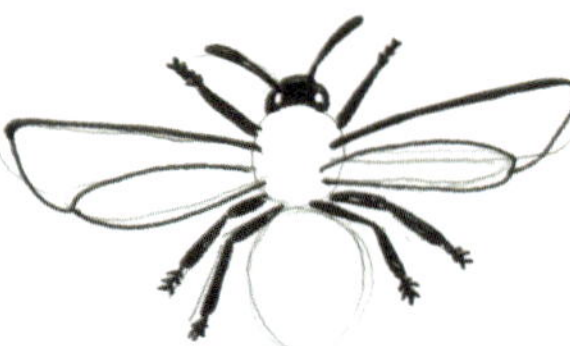 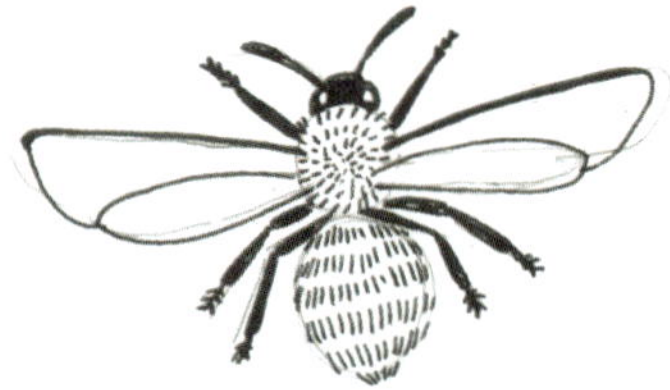 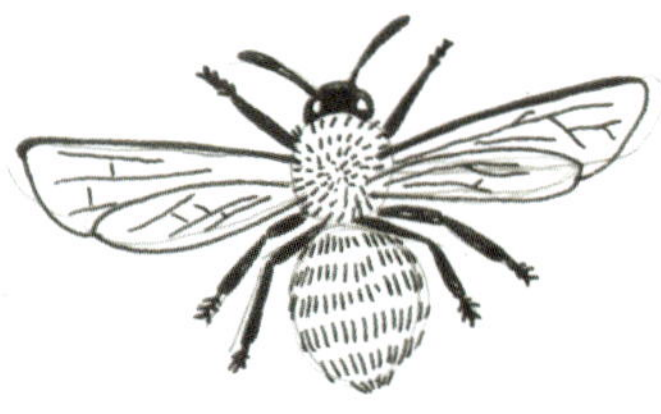

Trace the forewings and hindwings in ink. Make the top line of the forewing a bit thicker and darker than the rest.

Ink in tiny lines on the thorax and abdomen to represent hairs. The lines on the thorax go out in all directions. The lines on the abdomen are arranged in neat rows.

Draw in some detailed wing veins.

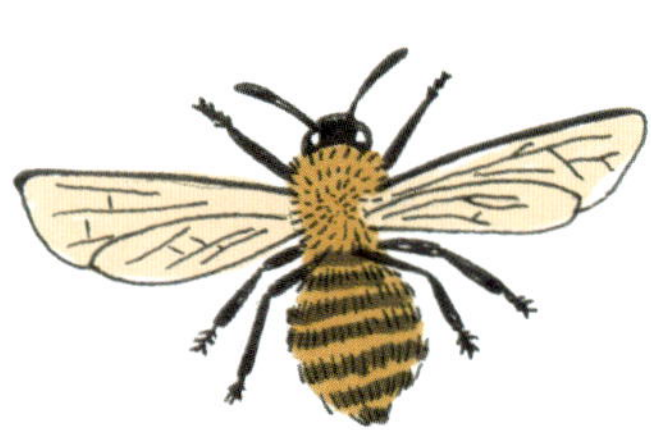

ANATOMY OF A BEE

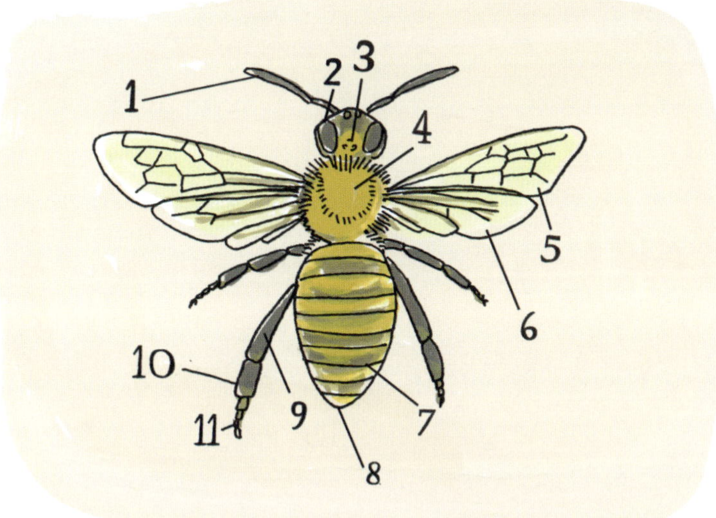

1. **antenna** - contains thousands of tiny sensors that detect smell
2. **compound eye** - for general distance sight
3. **ocellus** - an eye used for low light conditions in the hive
4. **thorax** - segment between head and abdomen where wings attach
5. **forewing**
6. **hindwing** — 2-part wings hook together in flight but separate at rest
7. **abdomen** - contains all the organs, wax glands, and stinger
8. **stinger** - only present on worker and queen bees
9. **femur**
10. **tibia** — three pairs of legs with six segments each;
11. **tarsal claw** used for walking and packing pollen

YEAR
MONTH

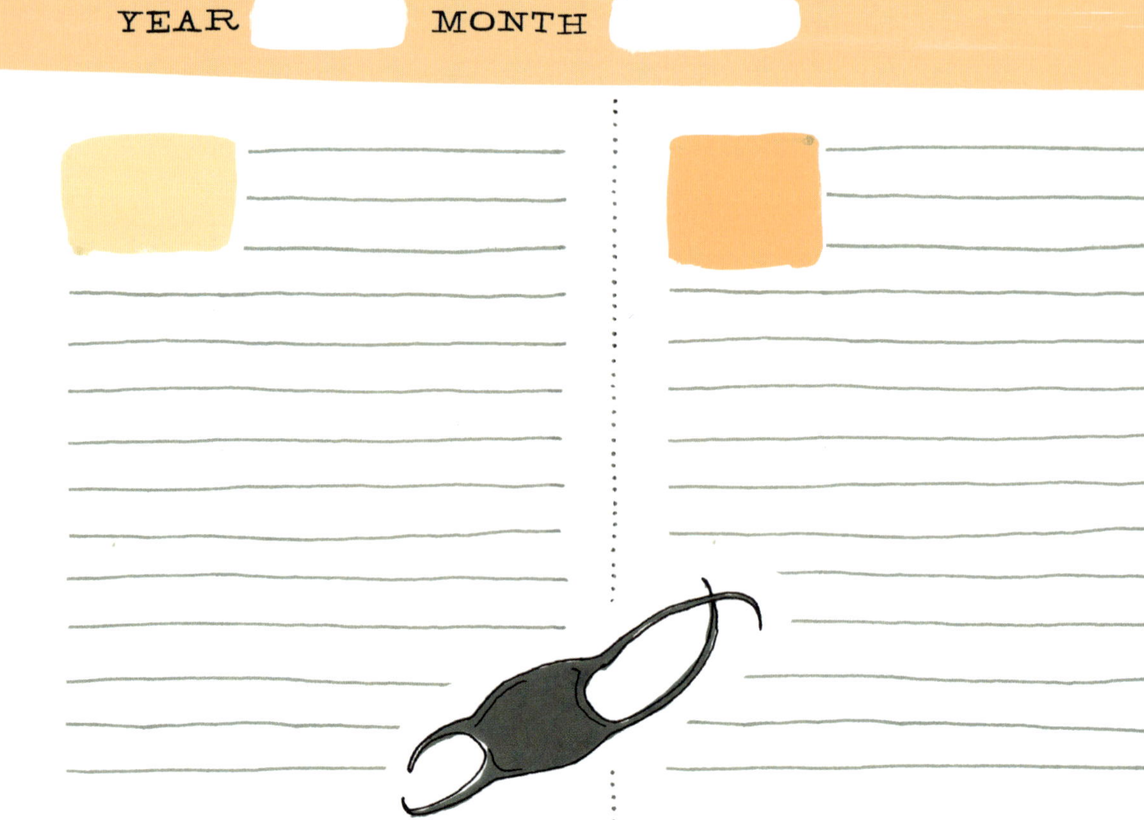

YEAR   MONTH

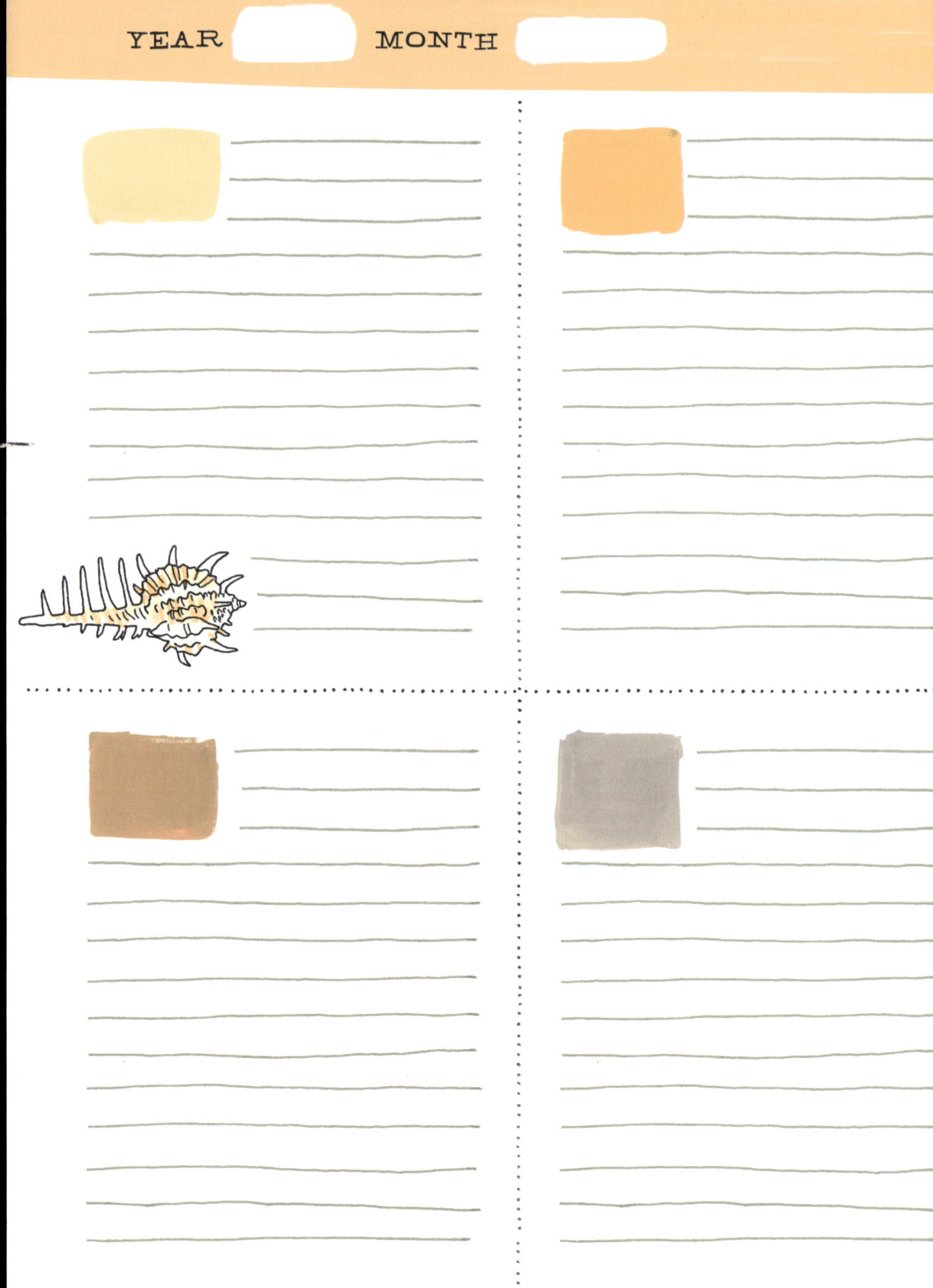

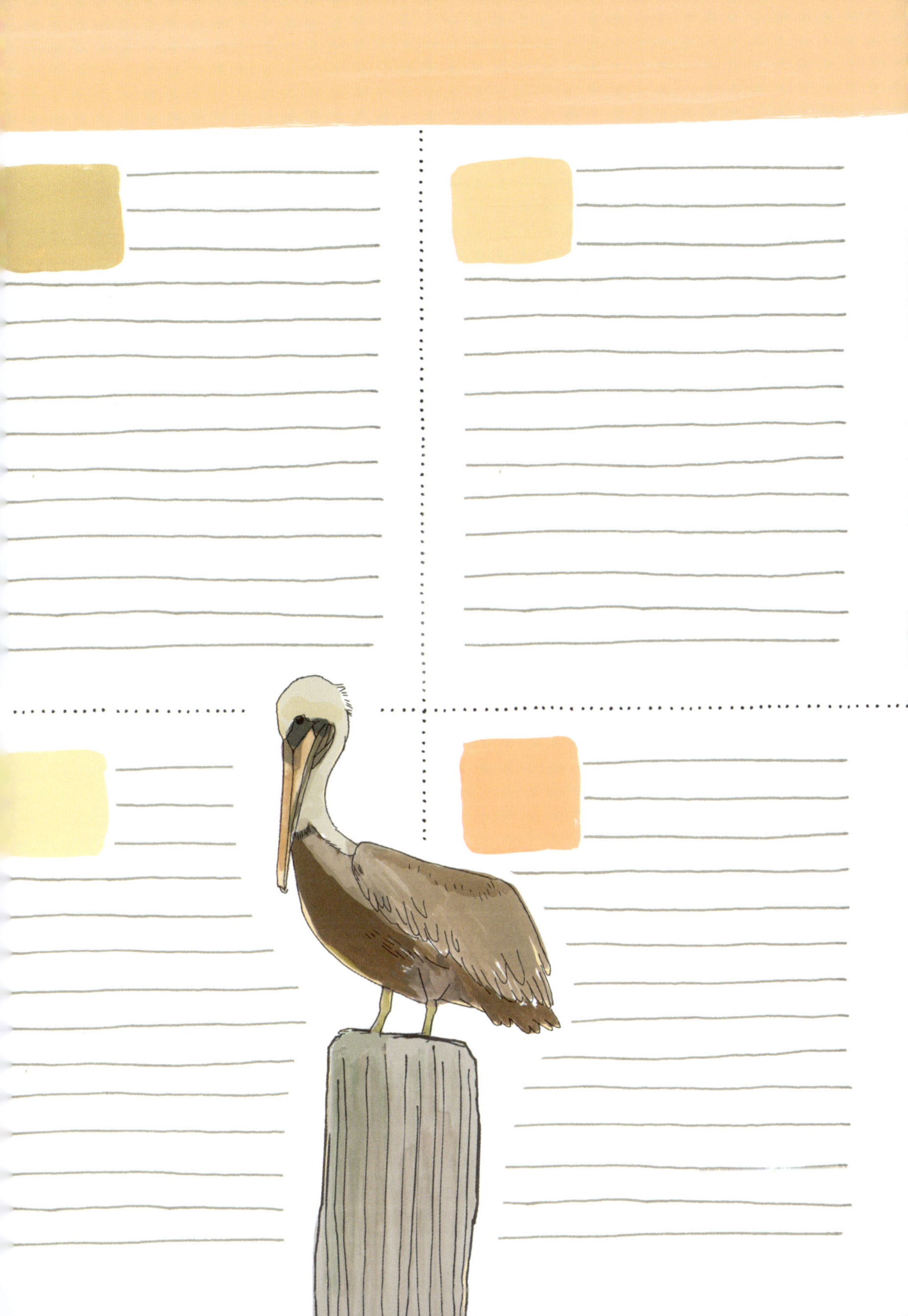

YEAR
MONTH

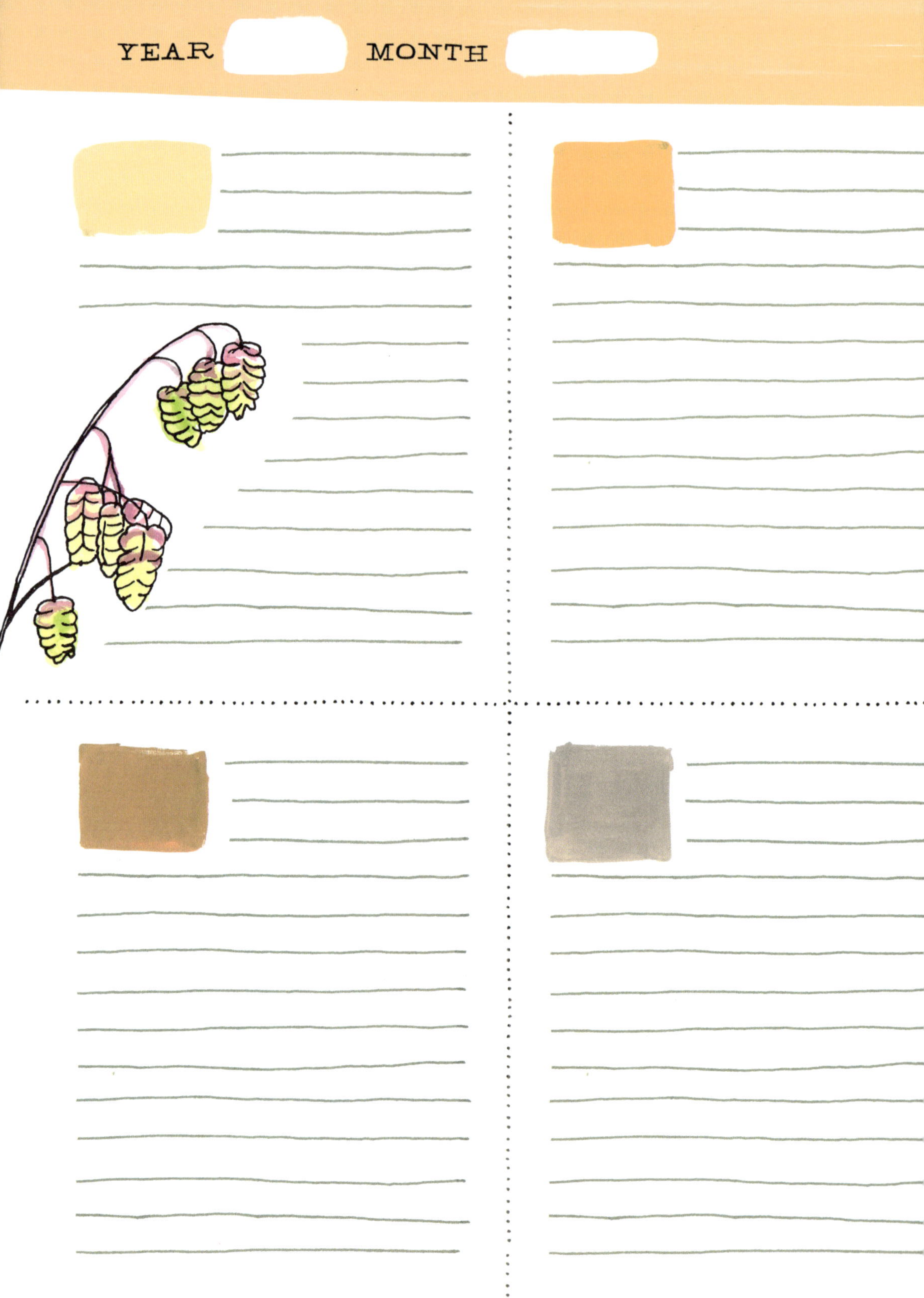

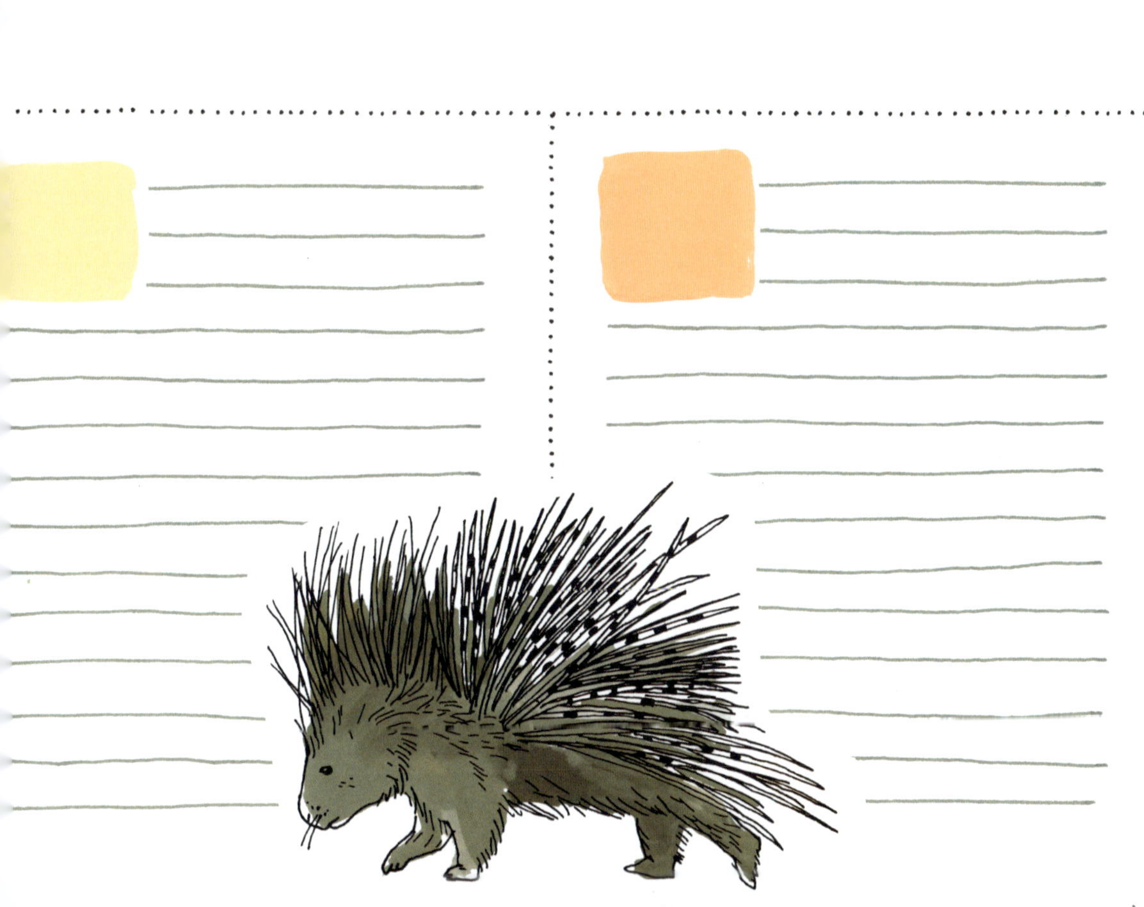

YEAR
MONTH

HOW TO DRAW A FLOWER

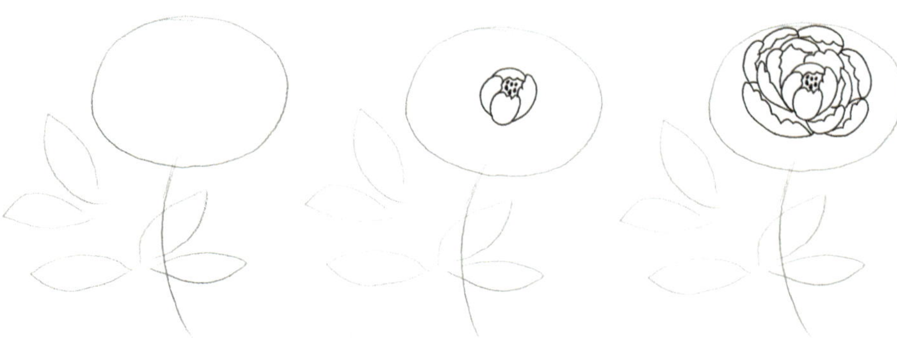

In pencil, sketch a circle for the outline of the blossom, a line for the stem, and roughly where the leaves will go.

In ink, start at the center of the blossom. Draw a few dots to represent the texture of the stigma. Then add a few petals surrounding it.

Work your way out in a cyclical pattern adding petals. For each petal, draw a smooth line on the outer edge and wavy line on the inner edge.

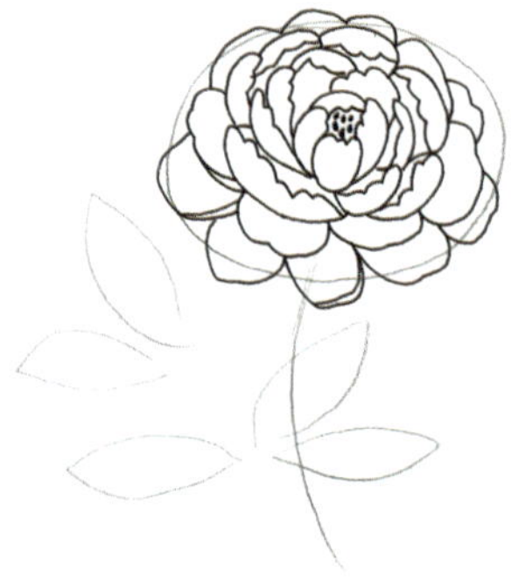

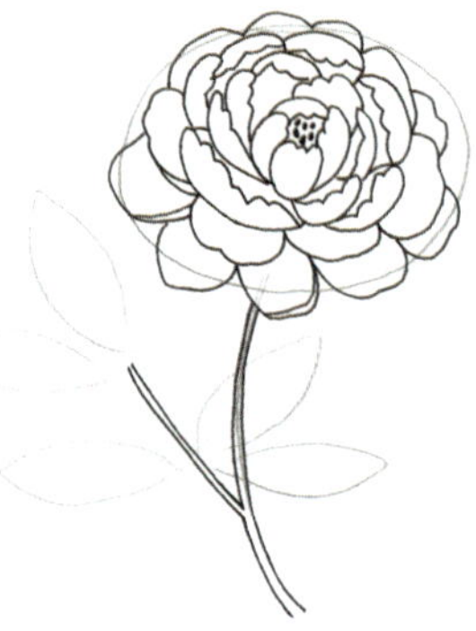

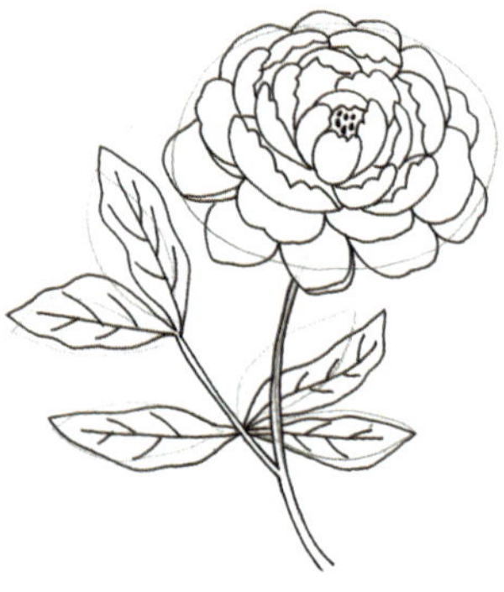

Add more and more petals radiating out from the center until you reach the perimeter of the circle you drew in pencil. The petals can get larger as you move away from the center.

Draw double lines for the stem and be sure not to cross the lines where the stem branches out.

Draw in each leaf over your pencil sketch, then add detail with thin lines for veins.

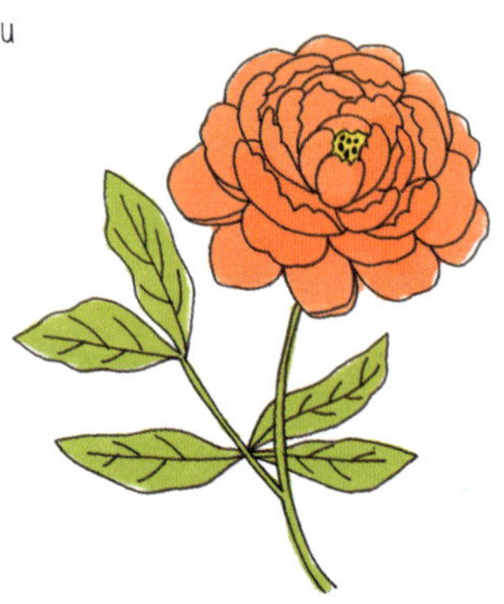

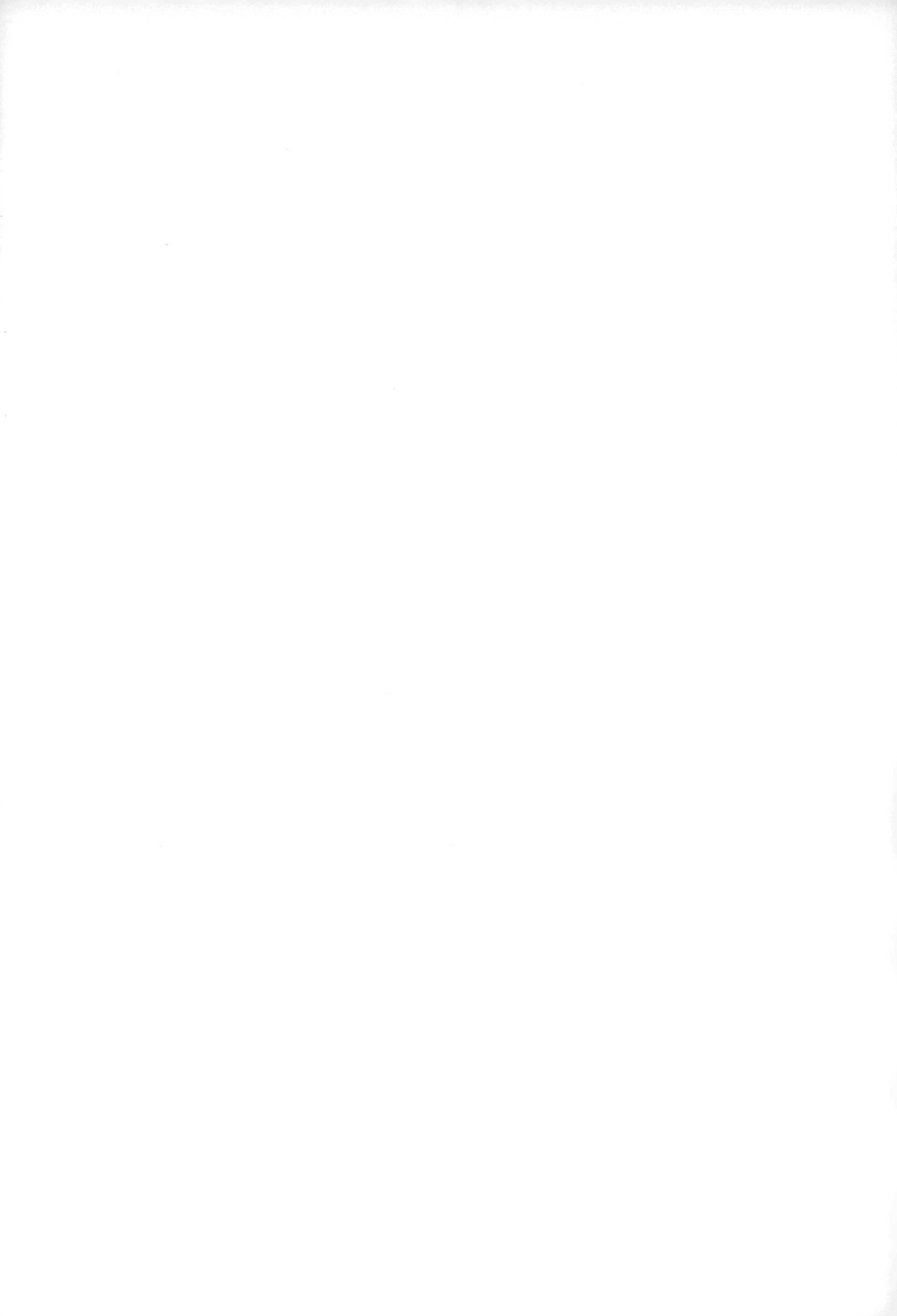

ANATOMY OF A FLOWER

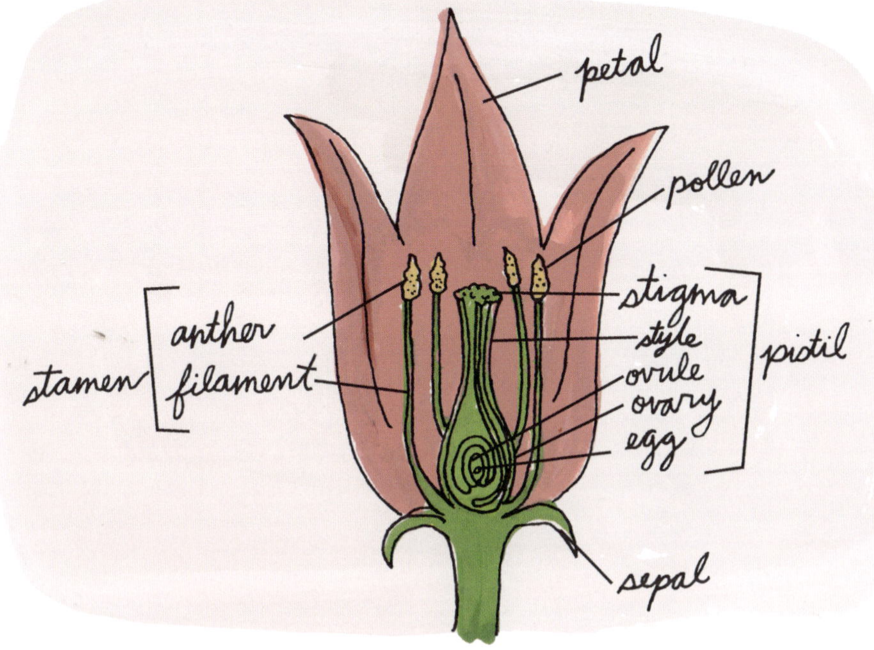

anther - male reproductive cell that contains pollen

filament - supports the anther

sepal - modified leaf beneath the flower

stamen - includes the male parts of the flower

pistil - includes the female parts of the flower

ovary - female reproductive organ

ovule - reproductive cell; forms the seed when fertilized with pollen

stigma - structure atop the ovary that receives pollen

style - stalk that connects the stigma and the ovary

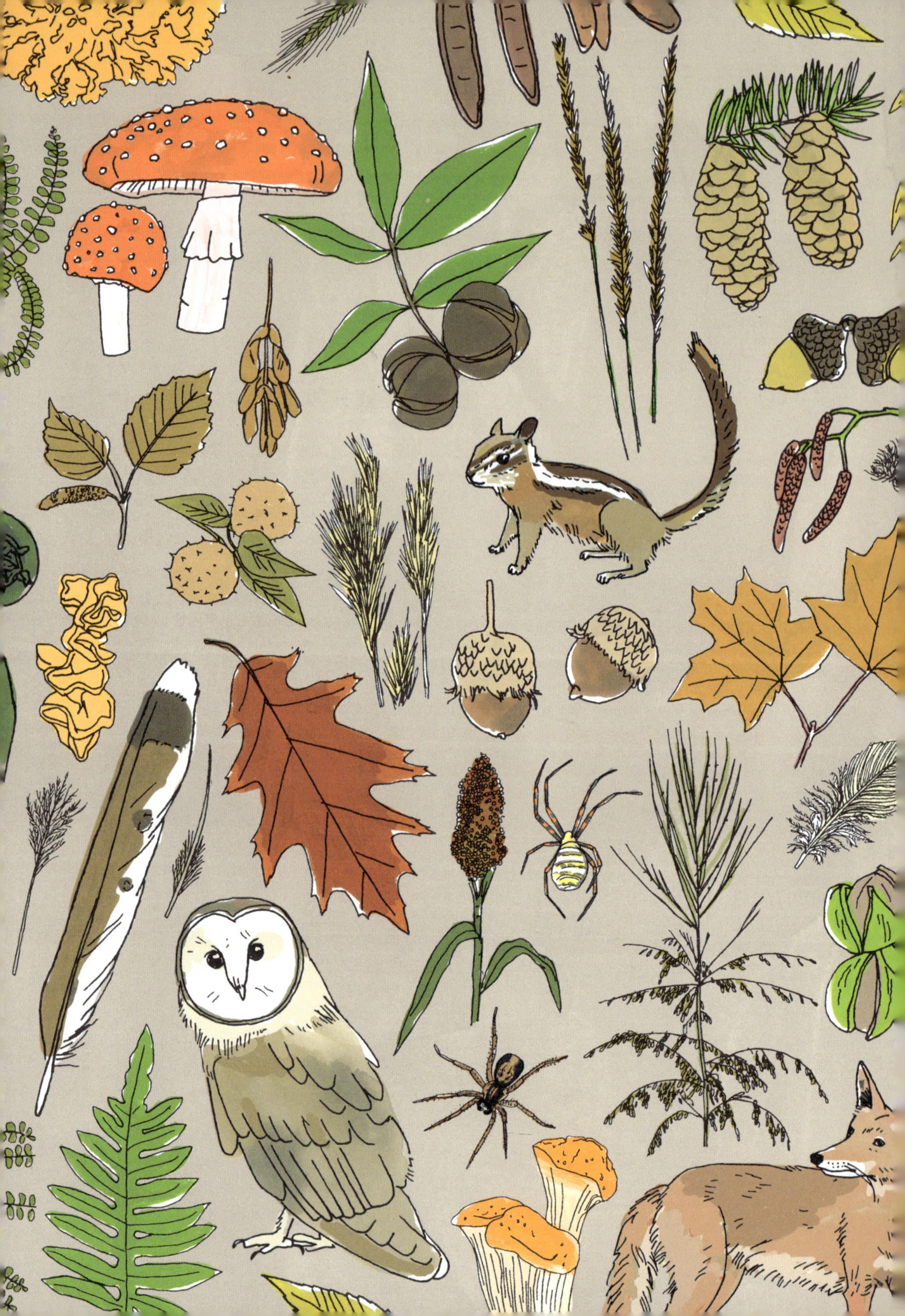

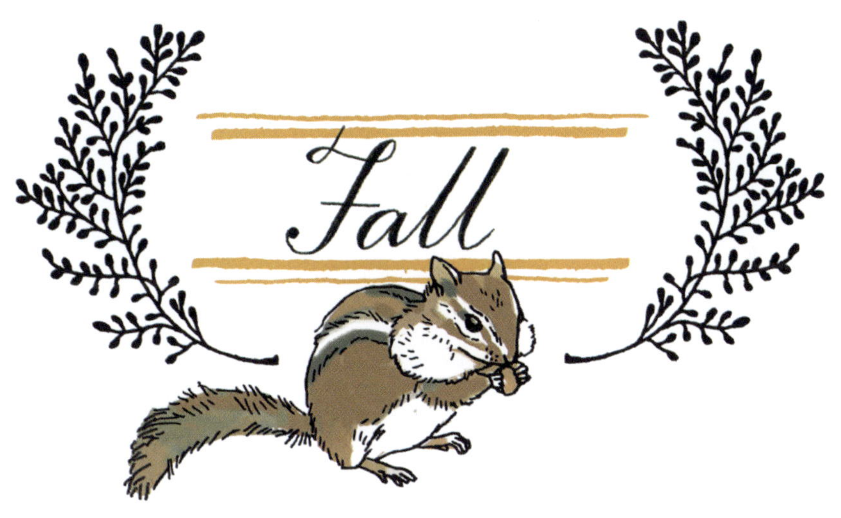
Fall

YEAR
MONTH

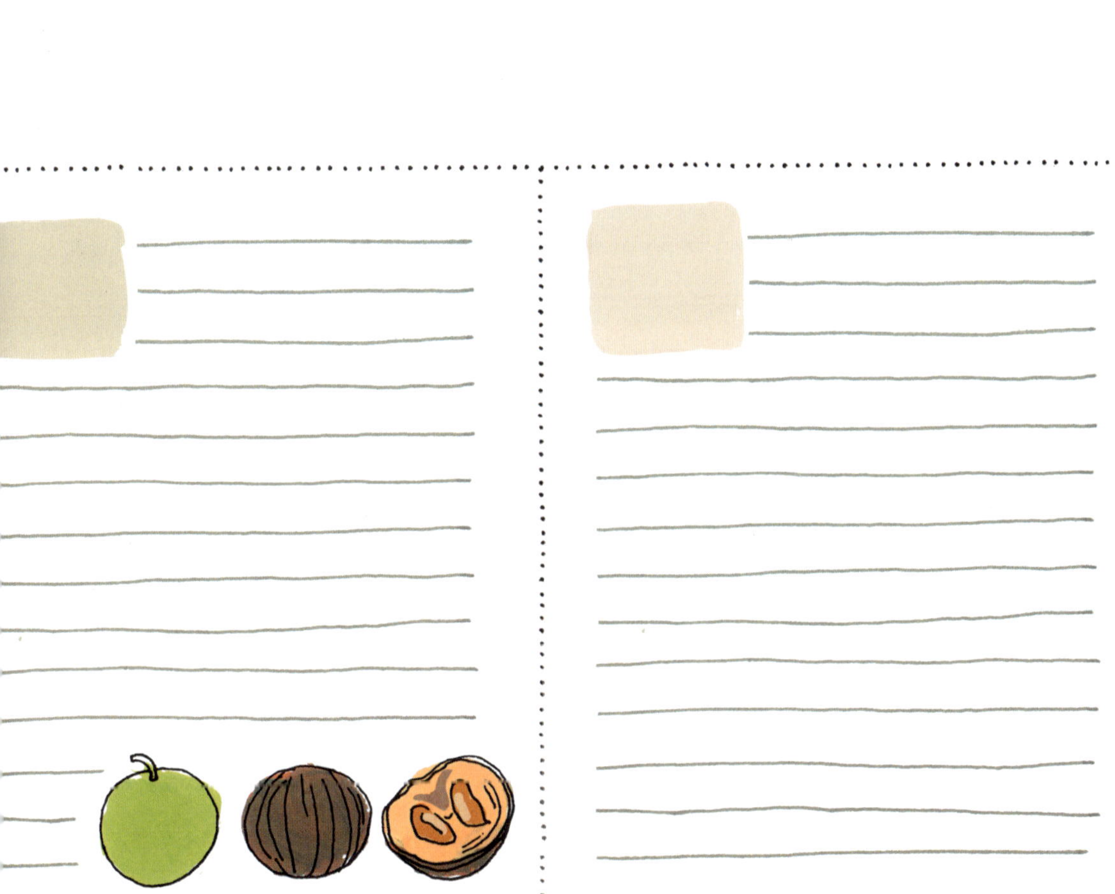

YEAR   MONTH

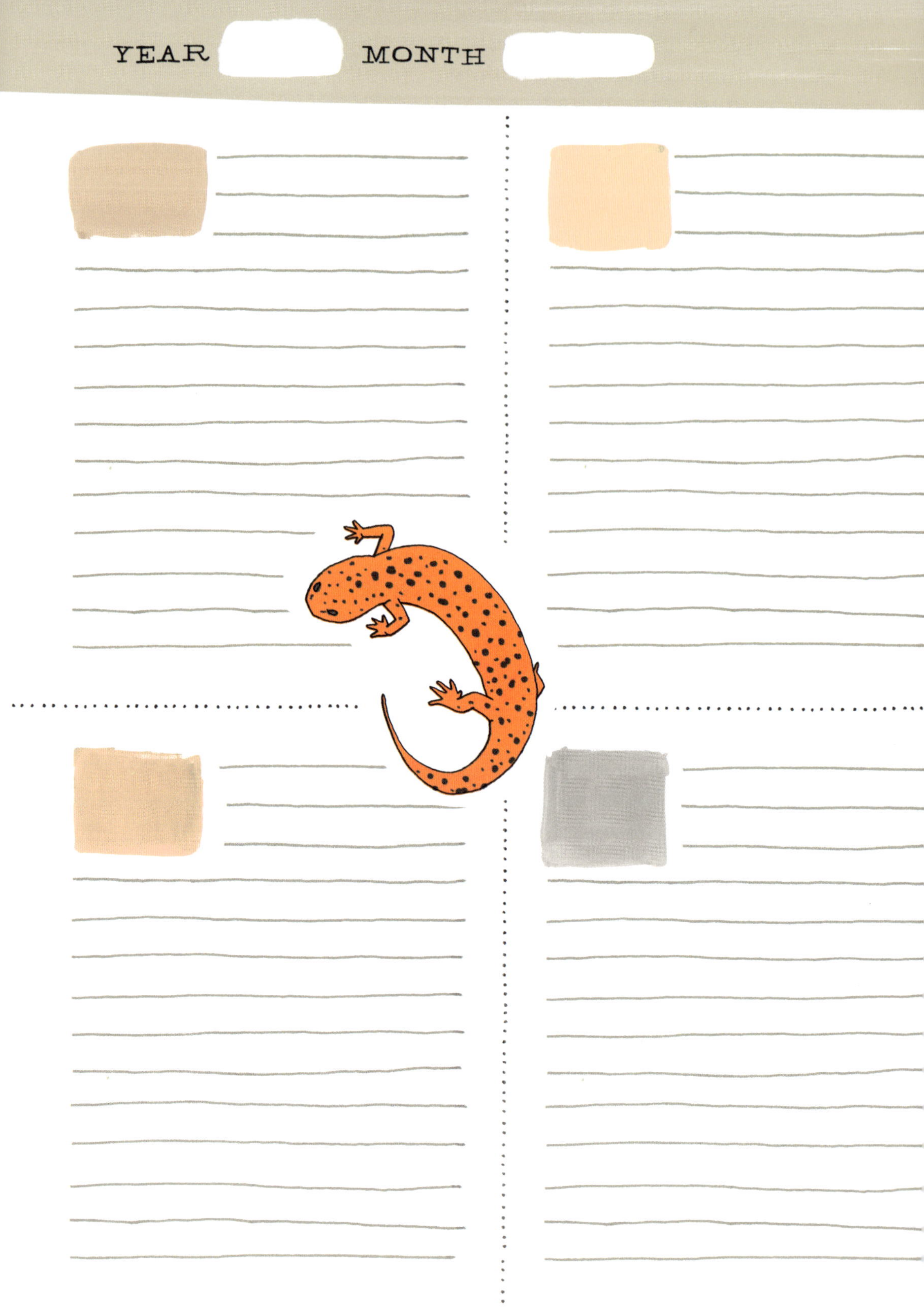

YEAR
MONTH

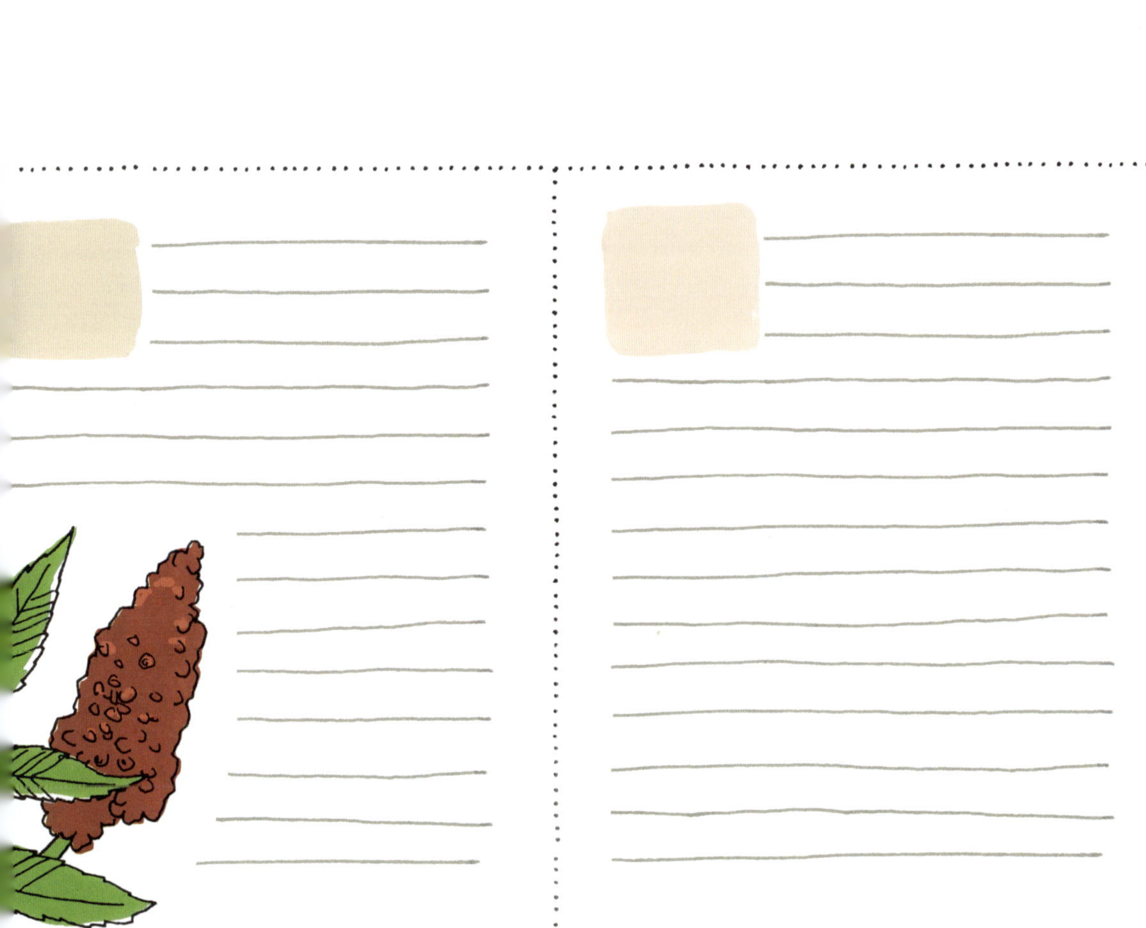

YEAR
MONTH

HOW TO DRAW A LEAF

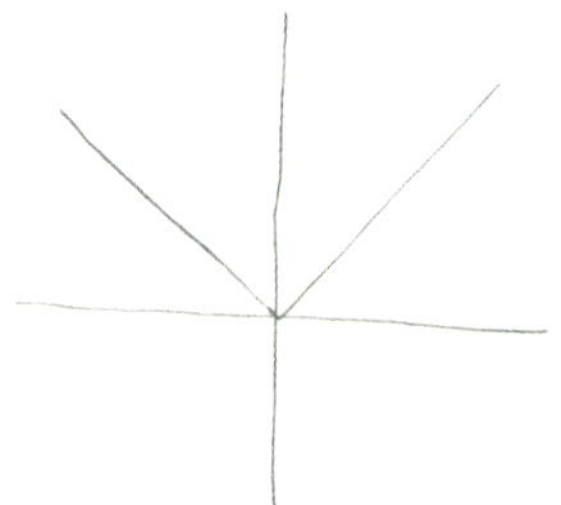 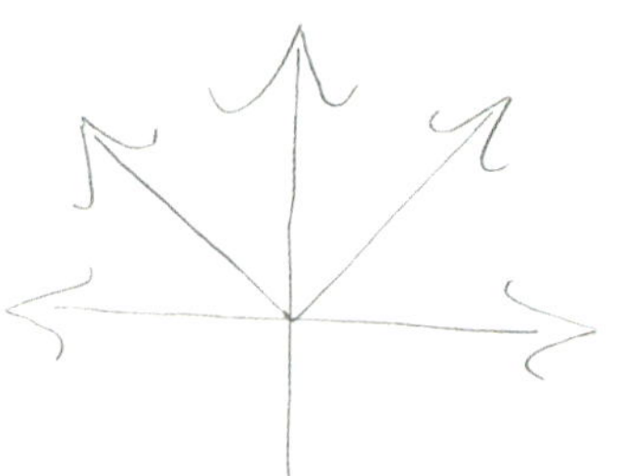 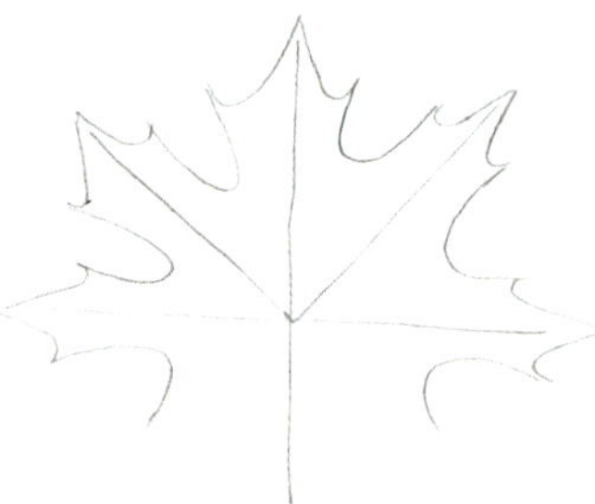

Draw a vertical line and an equal-size horizontal line that cross in the middle. Then add two diagonal lines that branch up from the intersection point.

Add arrowlike lines to the tops of the five upper lines. Make the arrow lines curve up at the ends.

Connect the arrow lines with big and little U shapes.

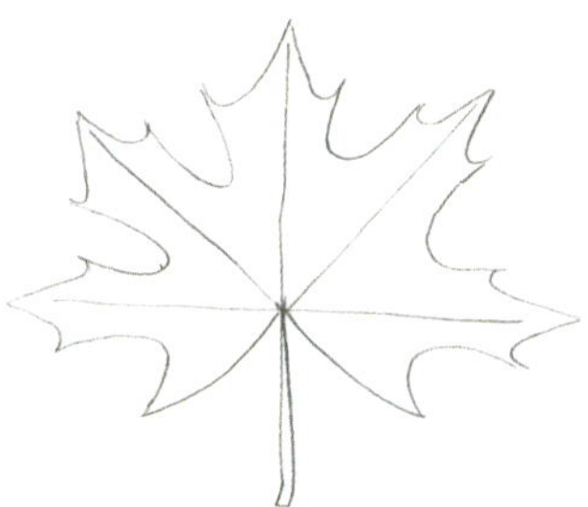 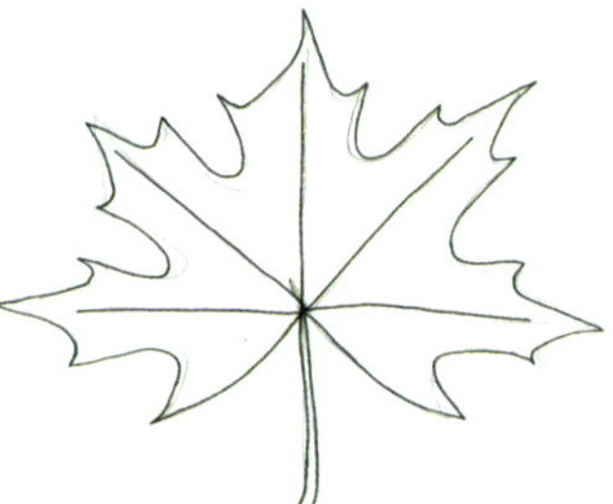 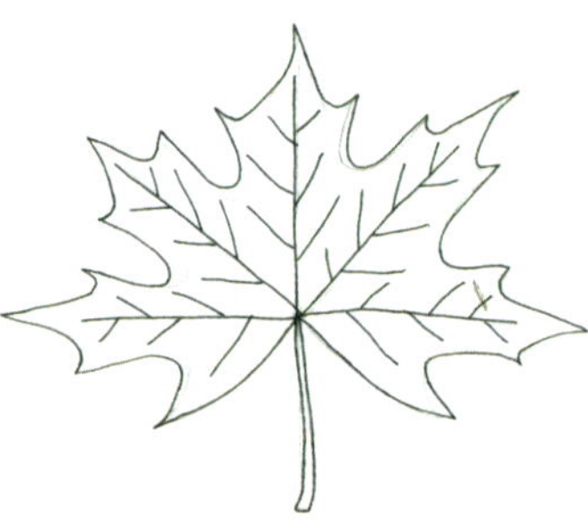

Draw in the stem, starting where the first two lines cross. Draw in the bottom of the leaf with two curved lines that meet at the top of the stem.

Trace over all the lines in ink.

Add vein lines branching out from the central lines.

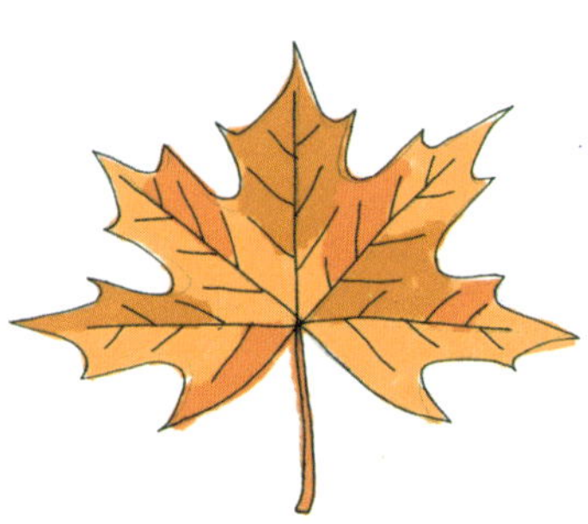

LEAF IDENTIFICATION

Shape

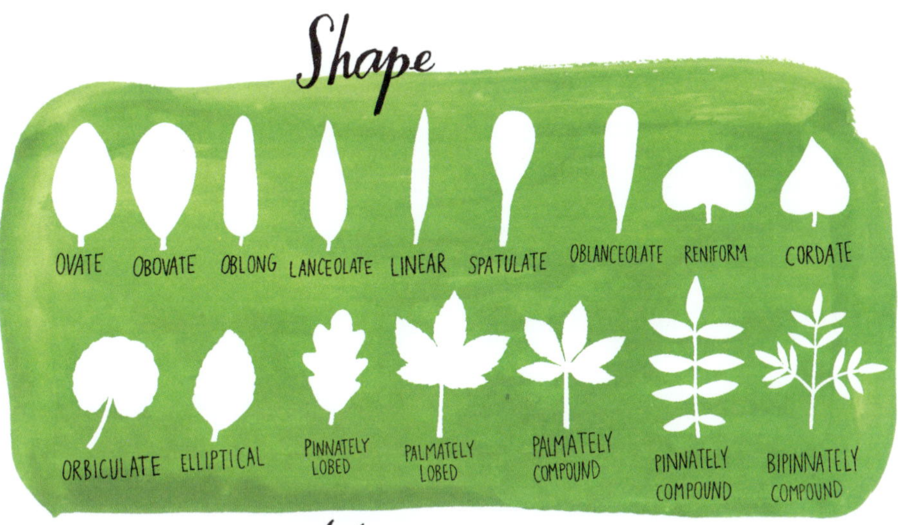

Margin (LEAF EDGES)

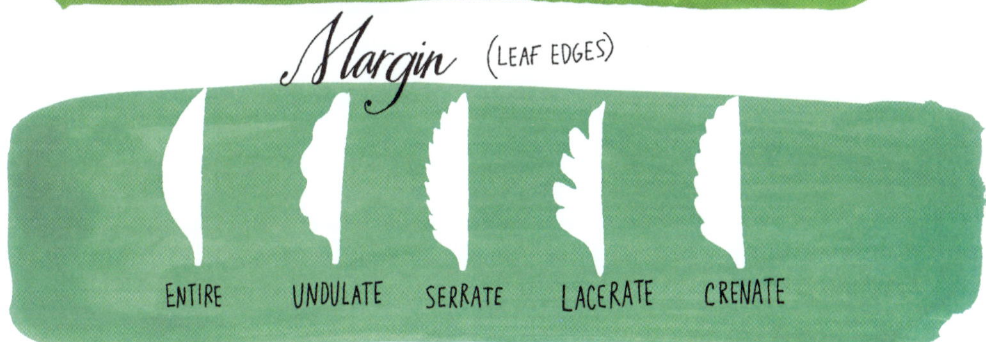

Venation (VEIN PATTERN)

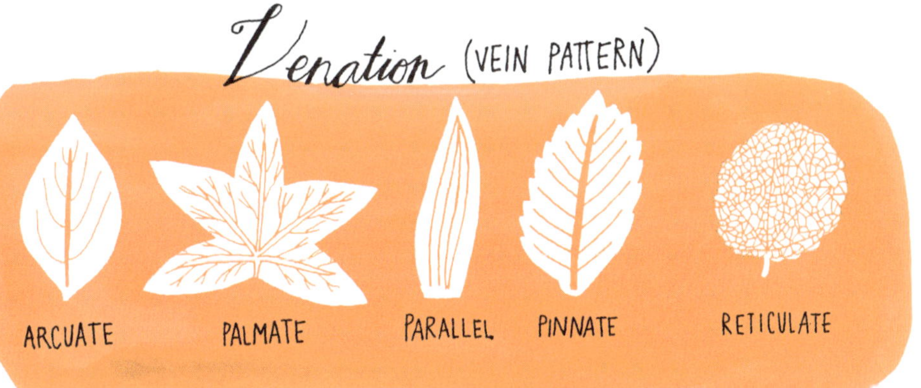

YEAR
MONTH

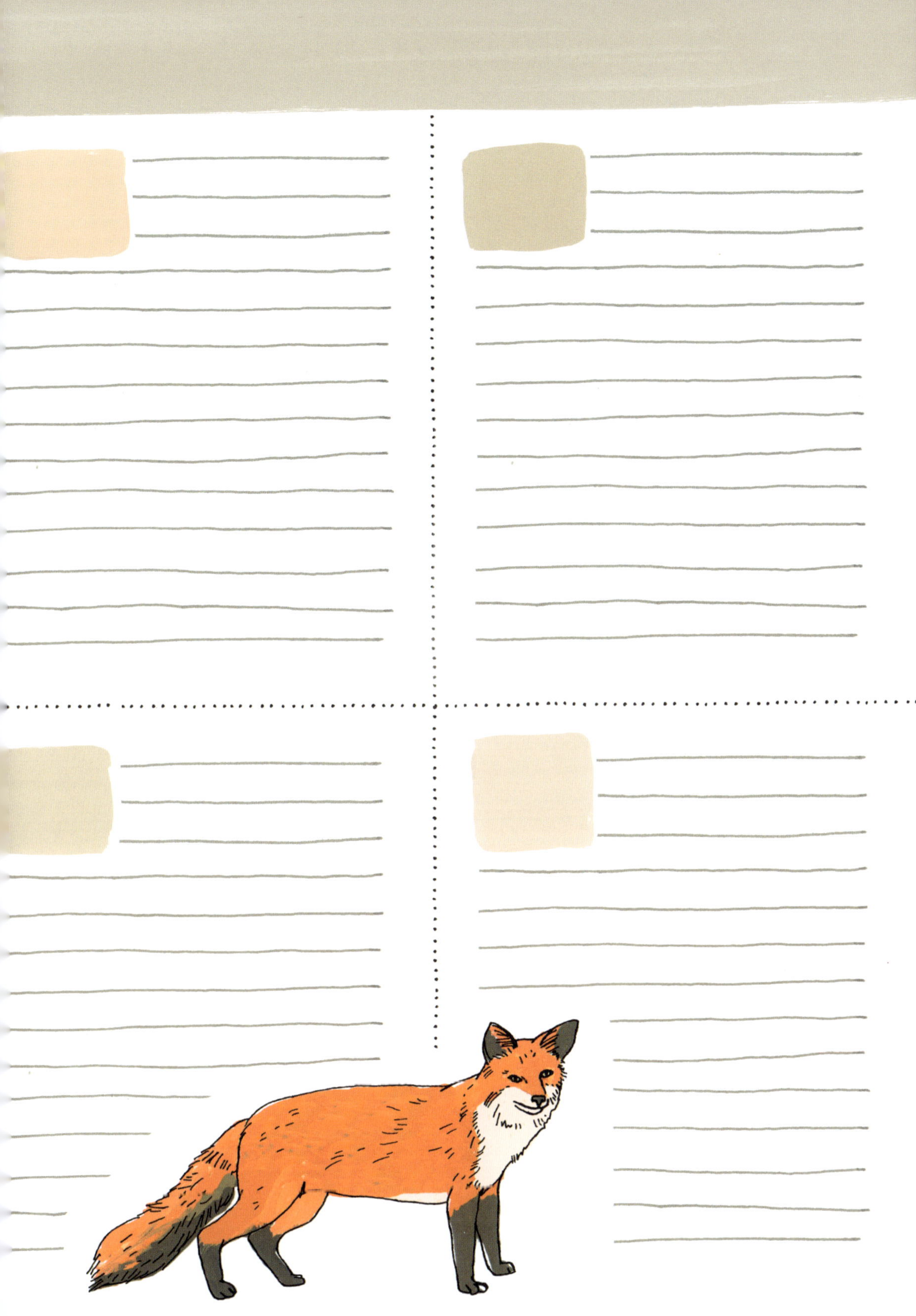

YEAR
MONTH

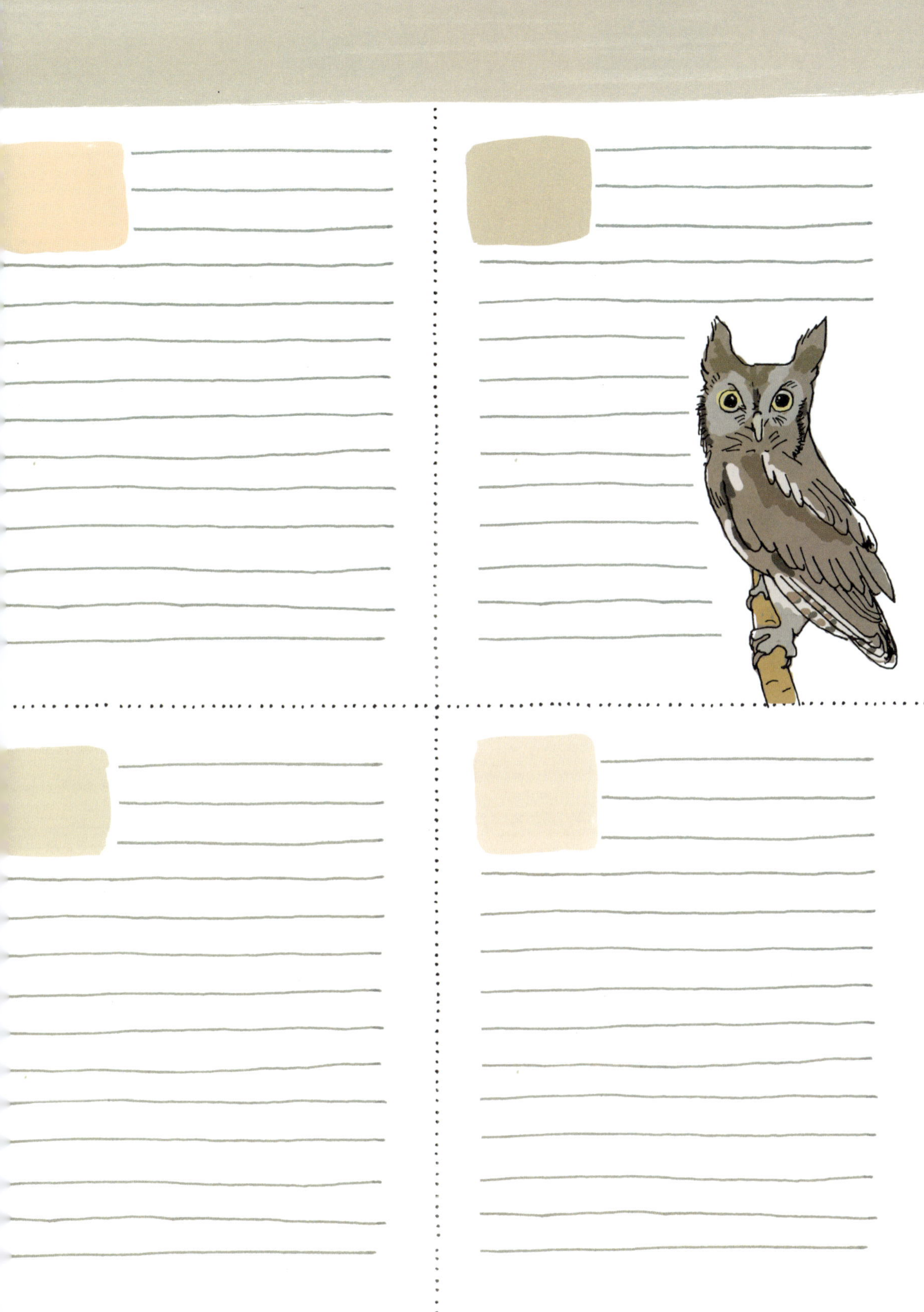

YEAR
MONTH

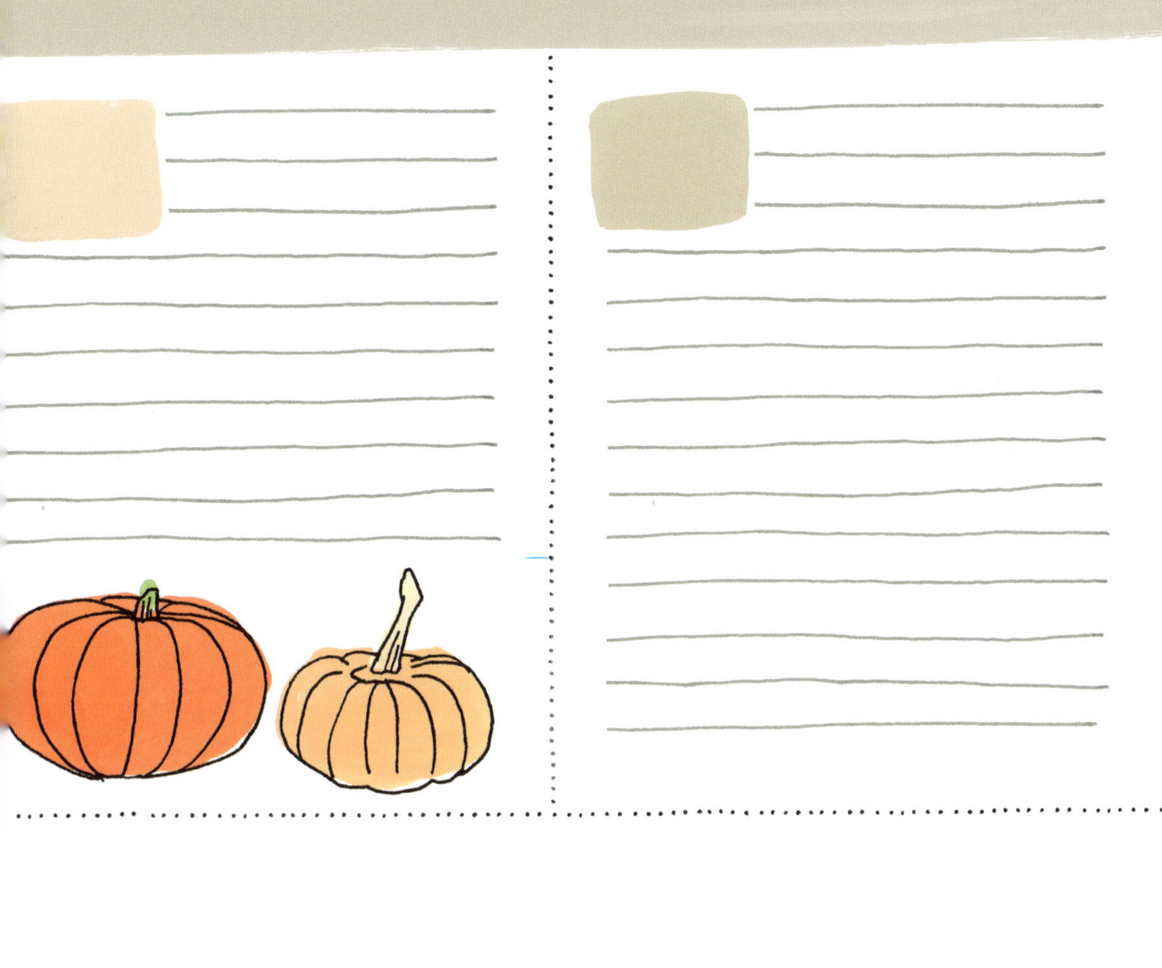

YEAR
MONTH

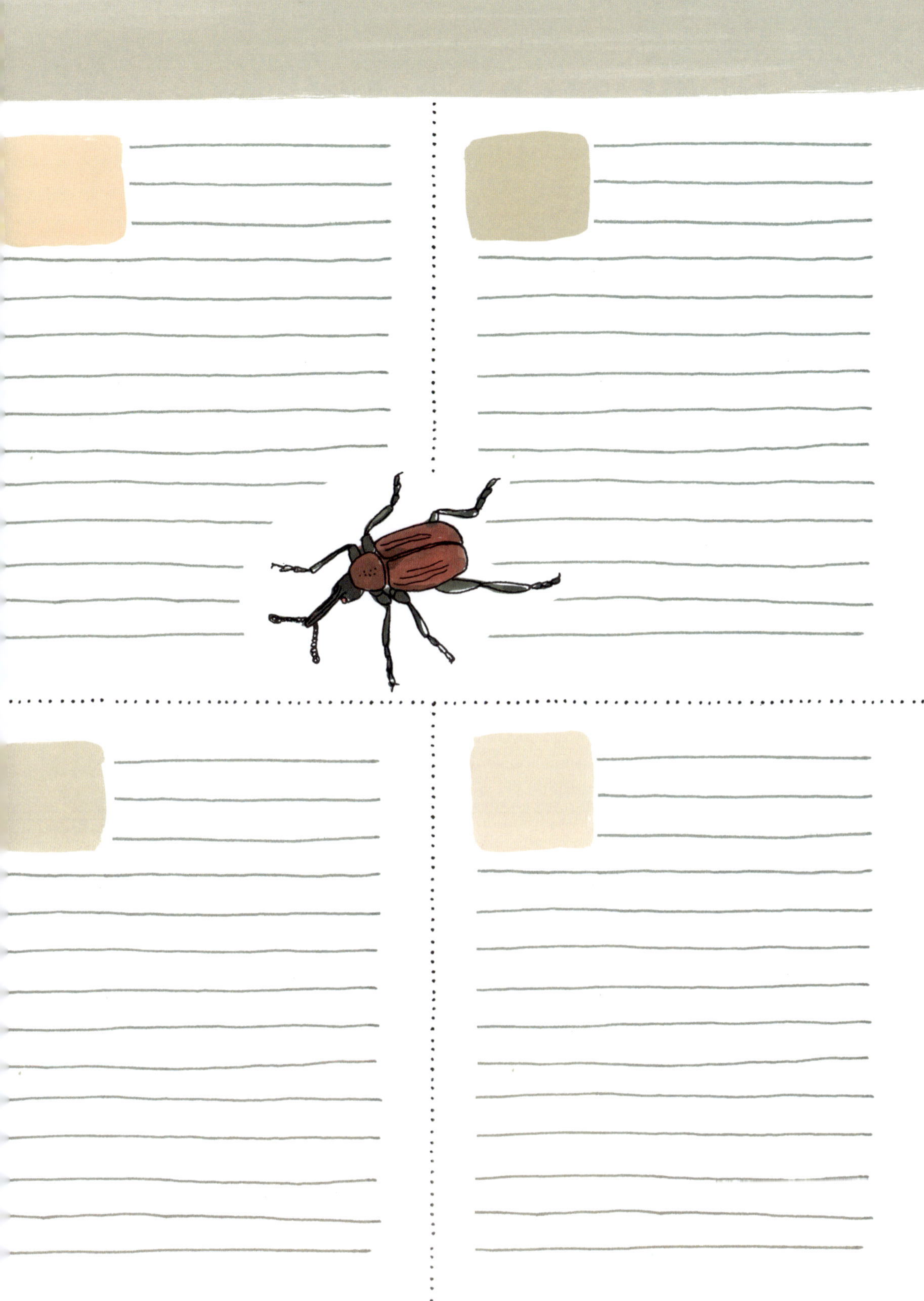

HOW TO DRAW A JELLYFISH

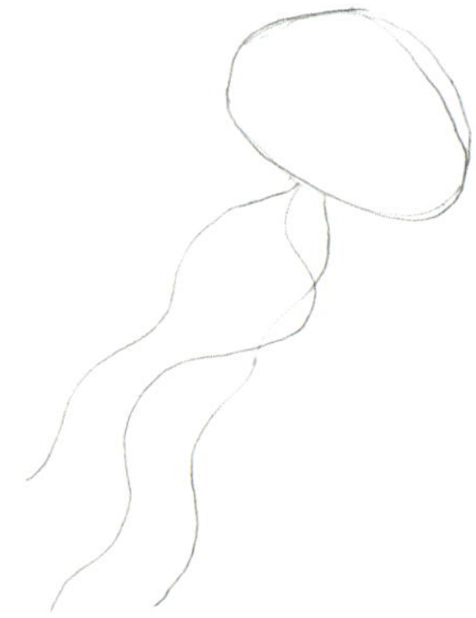

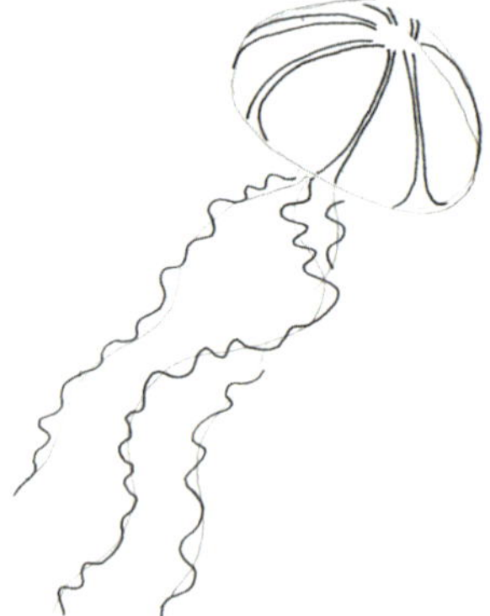

In pencil, sketch the body, also known as the bell, and the descending arms.

In ink, add canals to the bell. They will have a teardrop shaped appearance. And draw squiggly curving lines down each arm.

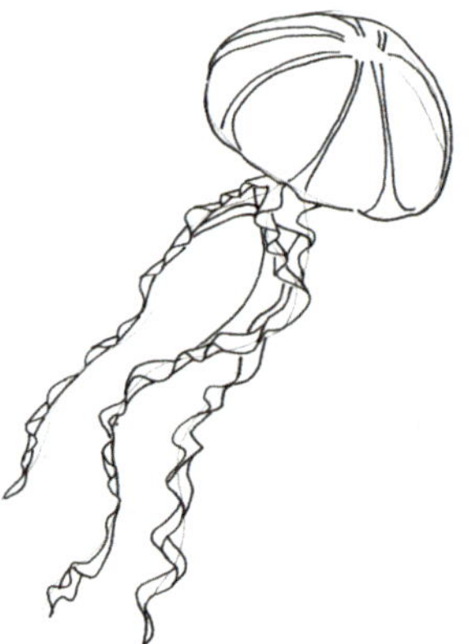

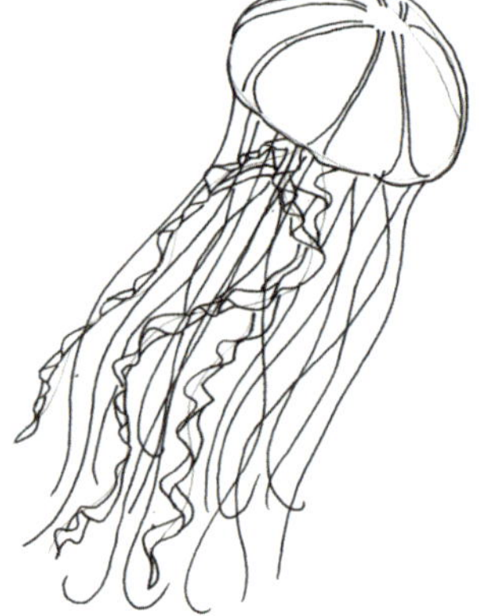

Draw the outline of the bell, and finish the arms by connecting each bump in the squiggly line to the descending arms.

Draw long, straight tentacles coming off the bell.

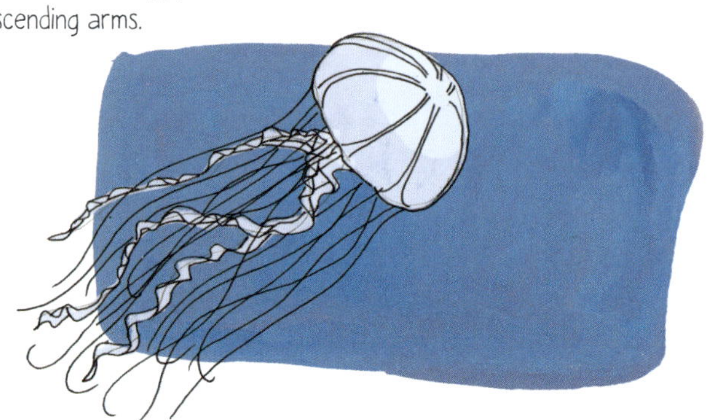

ANATOMY OF A JELLYFISH

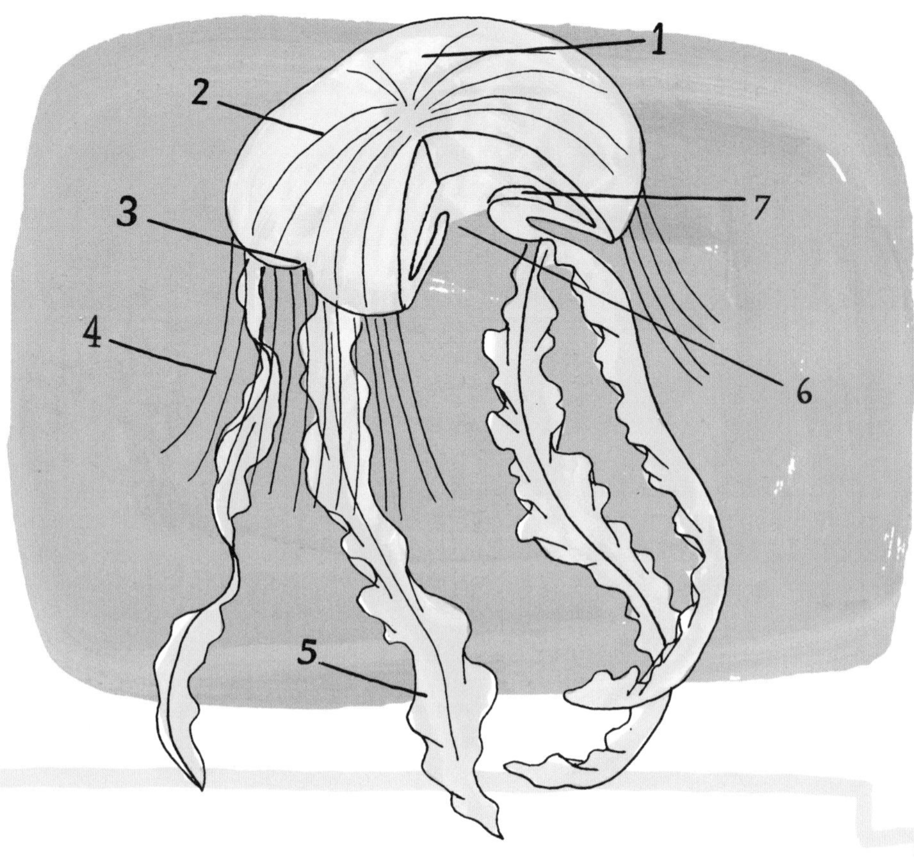

1. bell - umbrella-shaped body that contracts and expels water from the cavity underneath to propel the jellyfish

2. canal - a series of tubes that run along the bell to distribute nutrients throughout the body in what's called extracellular digestion

3. eyespot - light-sensitive spots on the rim of the bell

4. tentacle - used for touching

5. oral arm - injects the prey with venom

6. mouth - prey goes through here to the gastric cavity

7. gonad - reproductive organs that produce sperm and/or egg cells

YEAR
MONTH

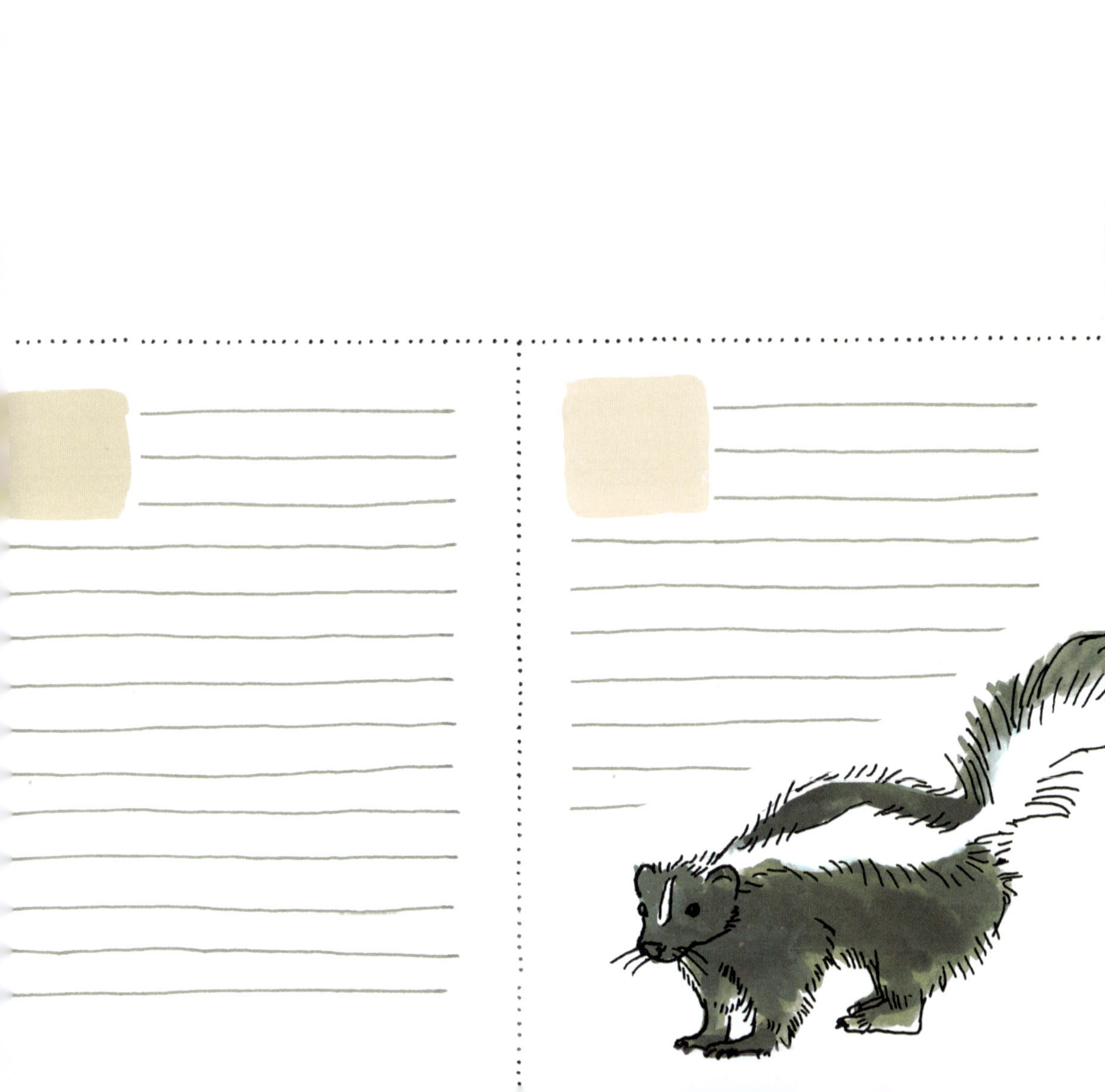

YEAR   MONTH

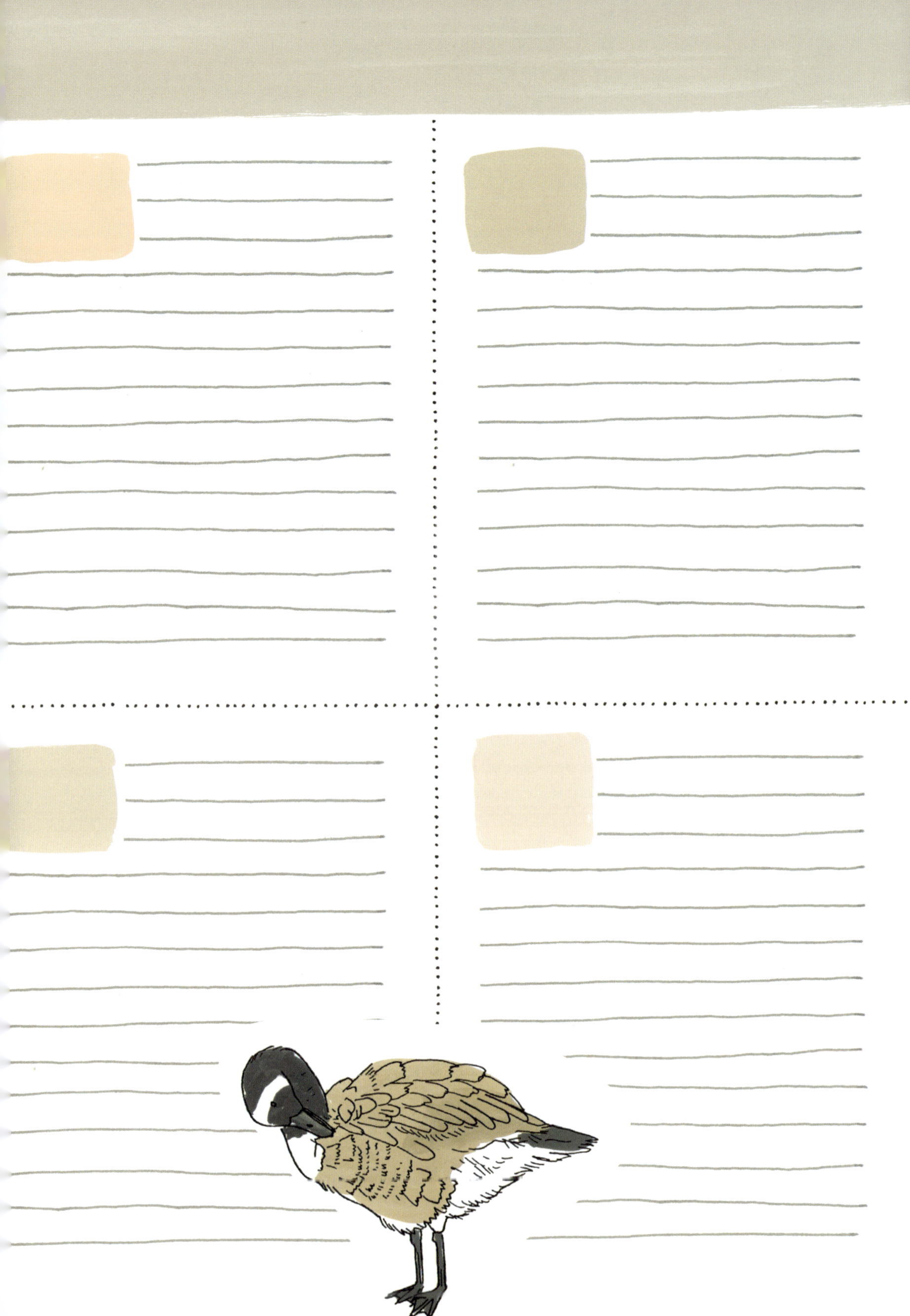

YEAR
MONTH

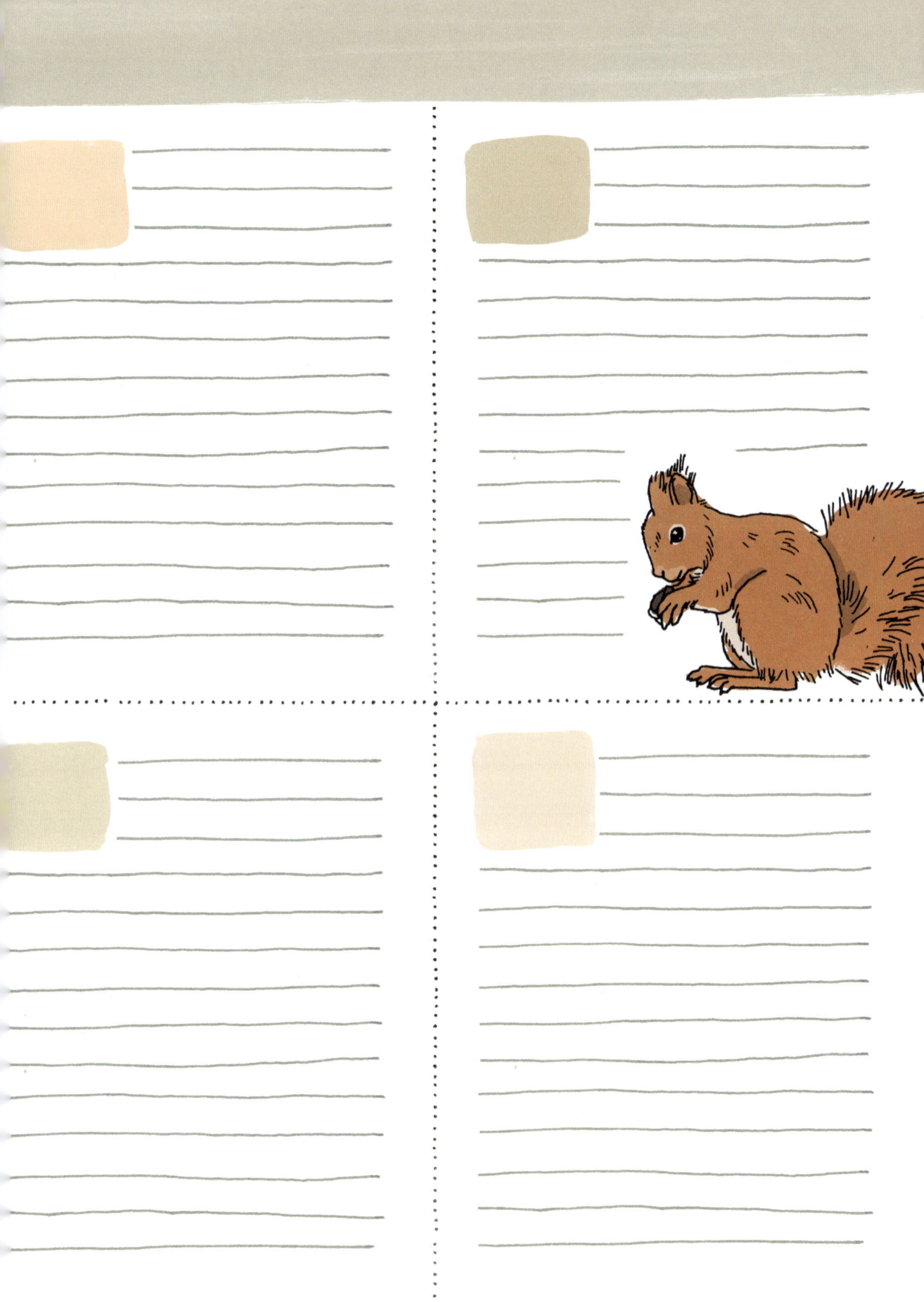

YEAR
MONTH

YEAR
MONTH

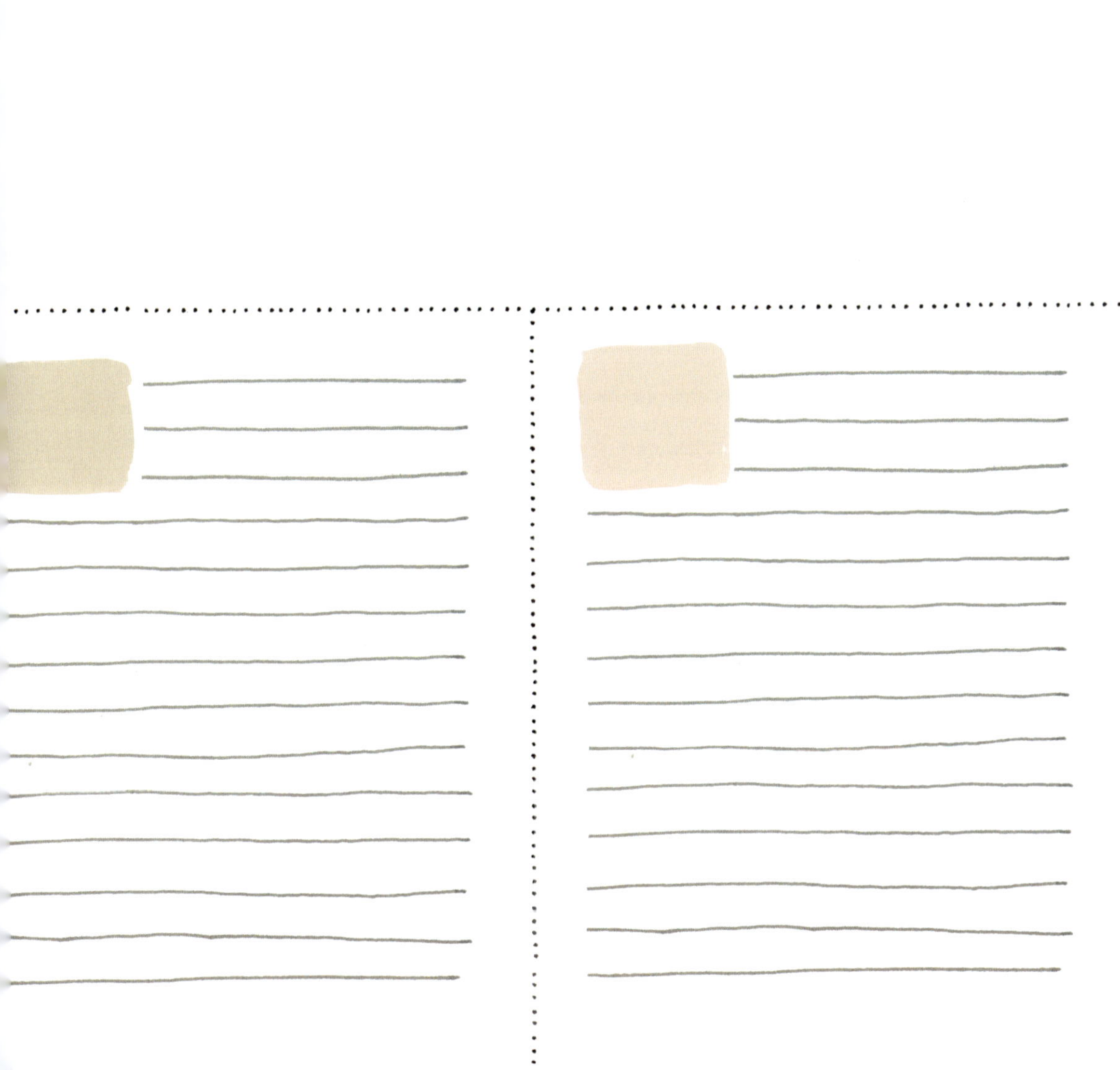

HOW TO DRAW A BRANCH

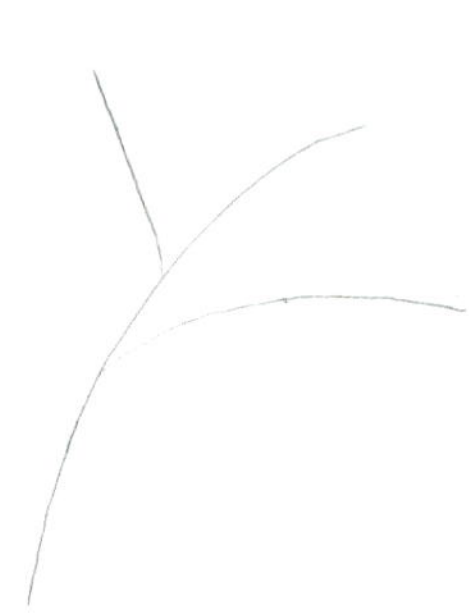 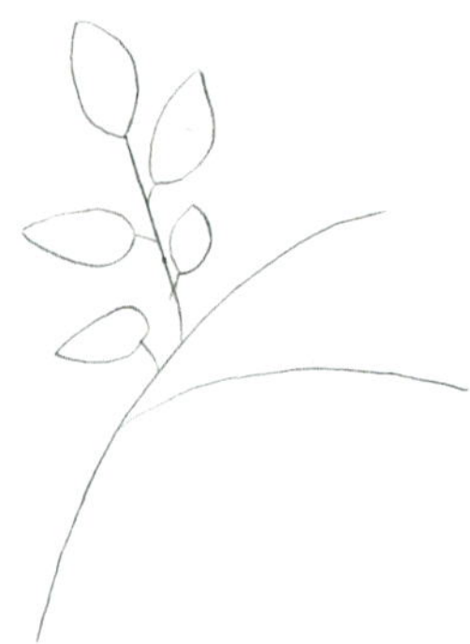 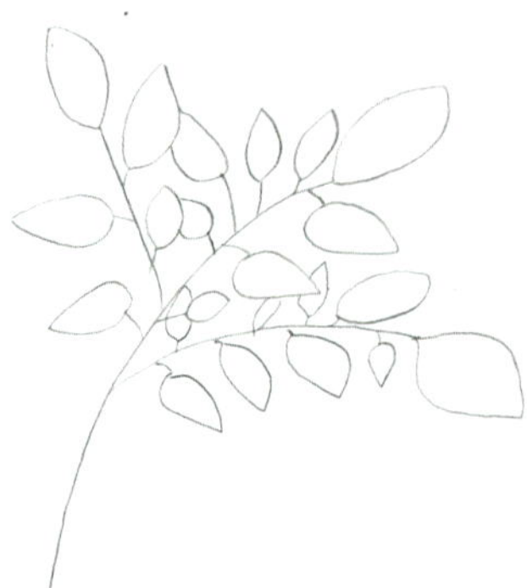

In pencil, sketch the main limb of the branch and a few off-shooting twigs.

Sketch in where the leaves will be on each twig.

Fill the twigs with leaves of varying sizes. Leaves tend to be smaller closer to the main limb and get bigger as they move out.

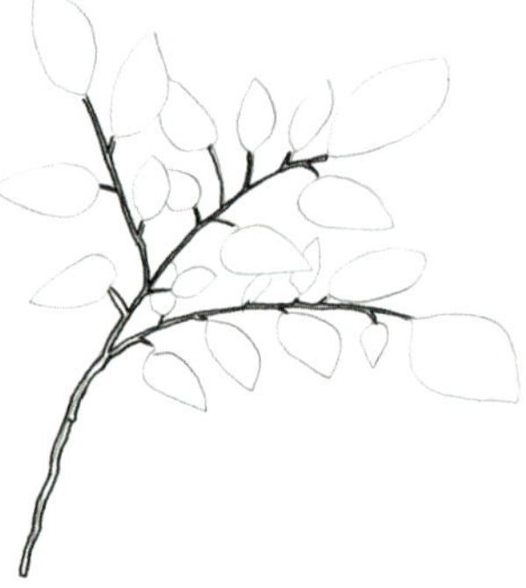 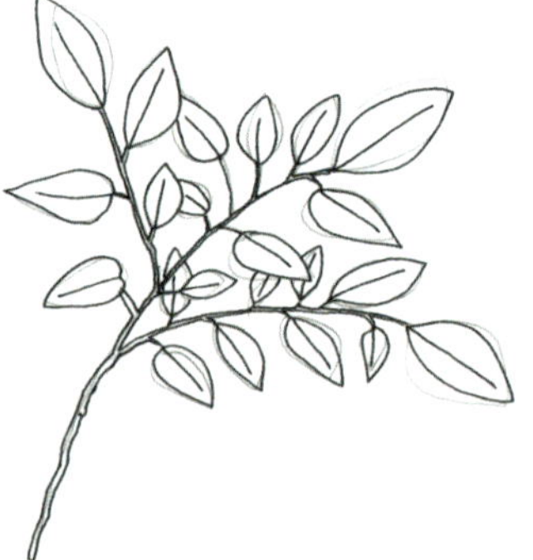

In ink, draw in the main limb and the twigs. Make the lines a little bumpy so they look natural.

Draw in the leaves and add leaf veins for detail.

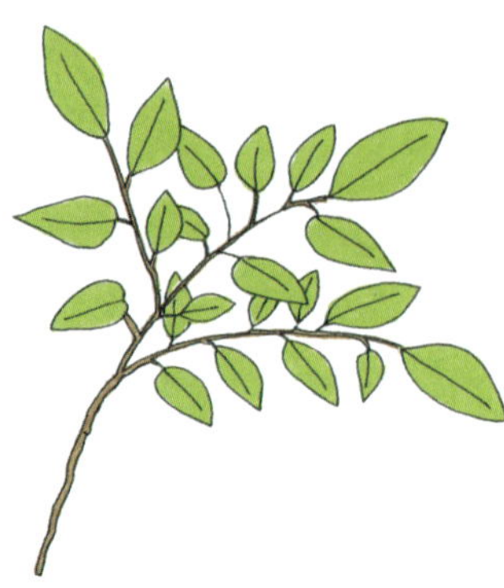

ANATOMY OF A DECIDUOUS TREE

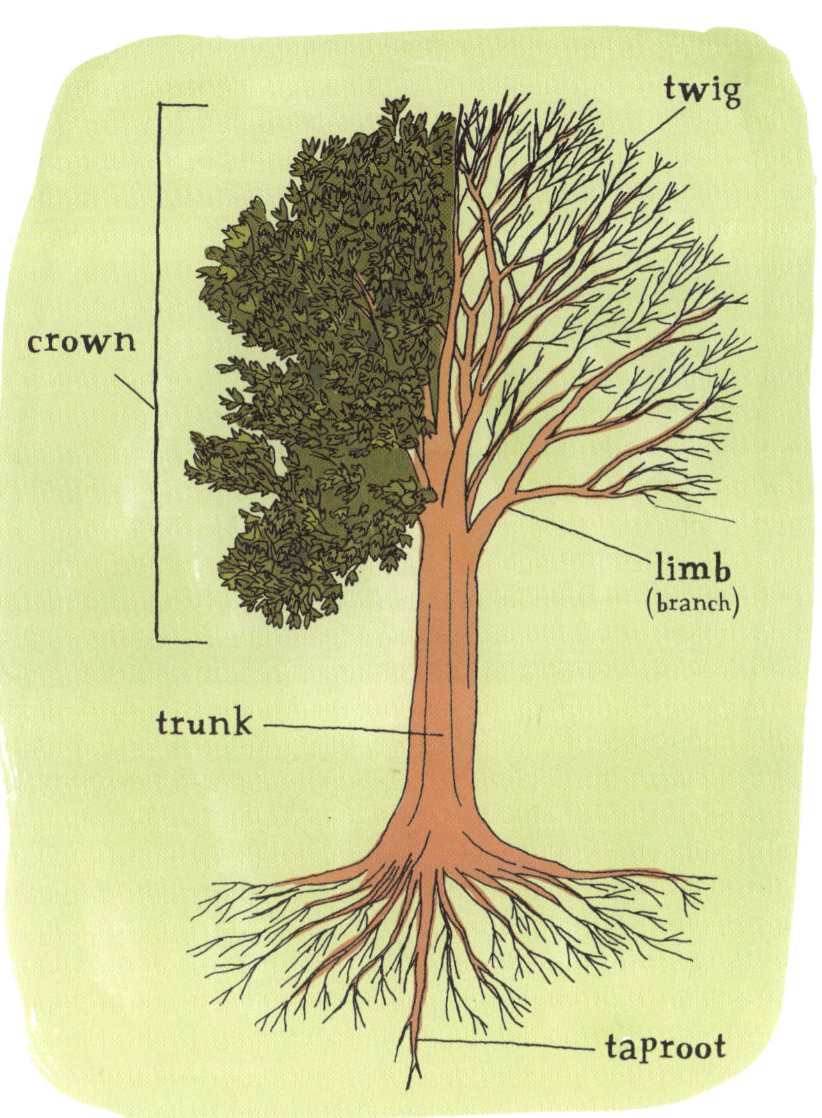

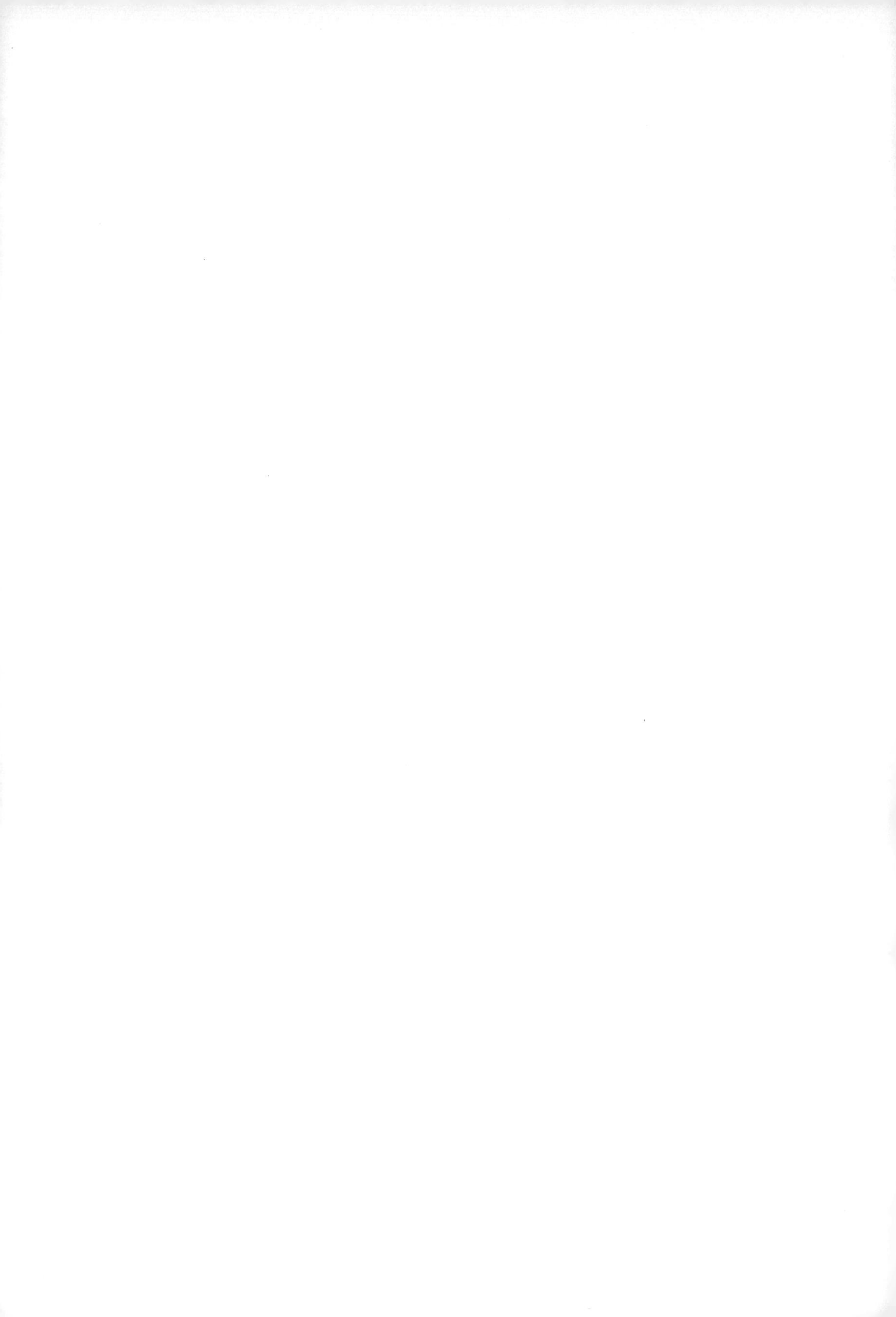

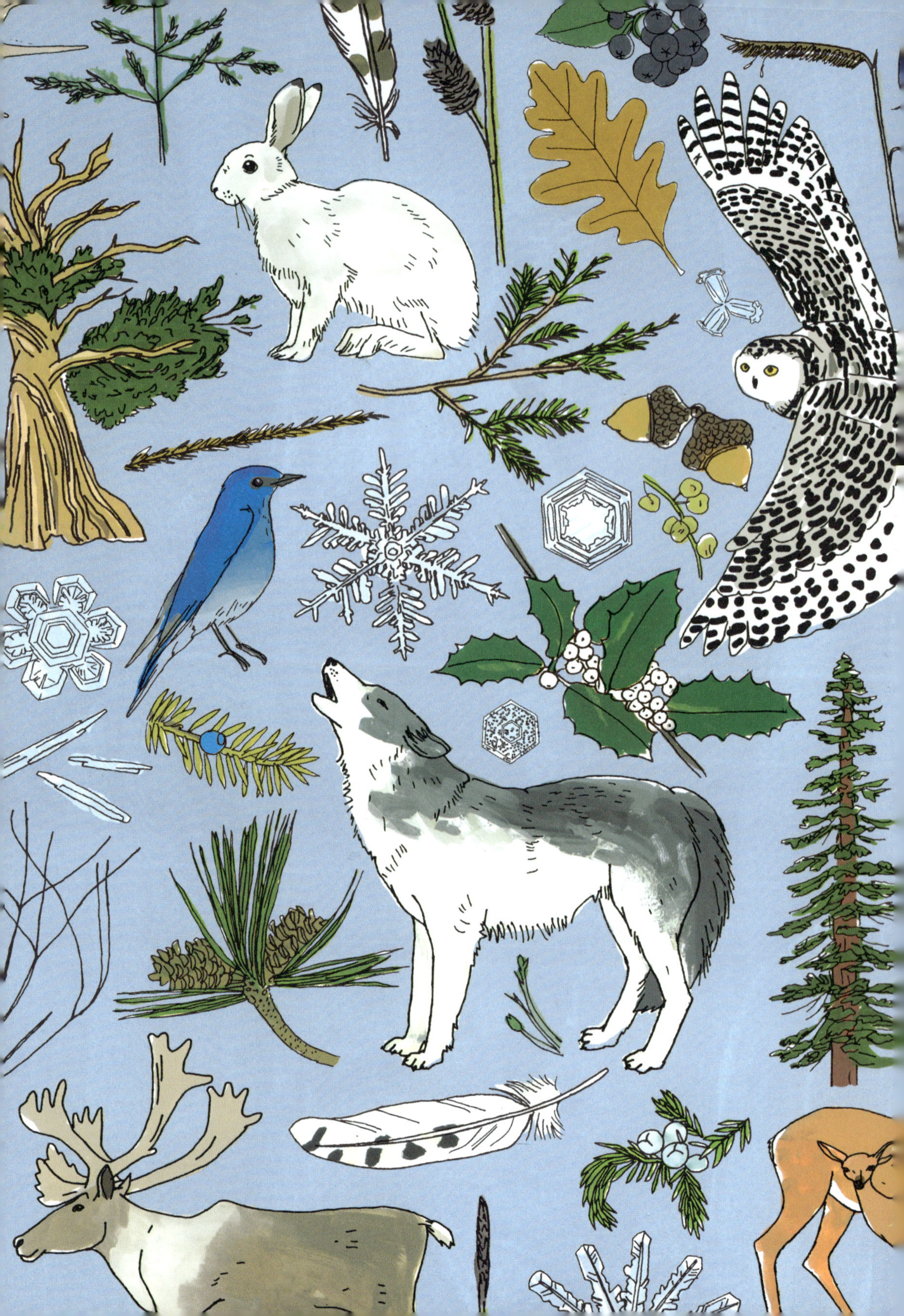

Winter

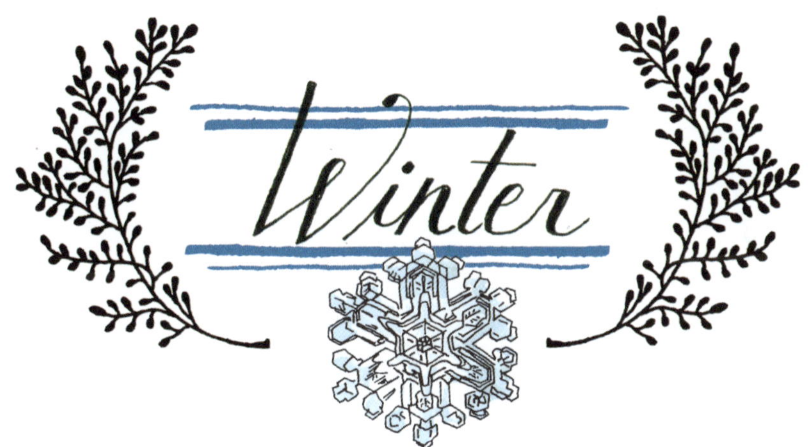

YEAR
MONTH

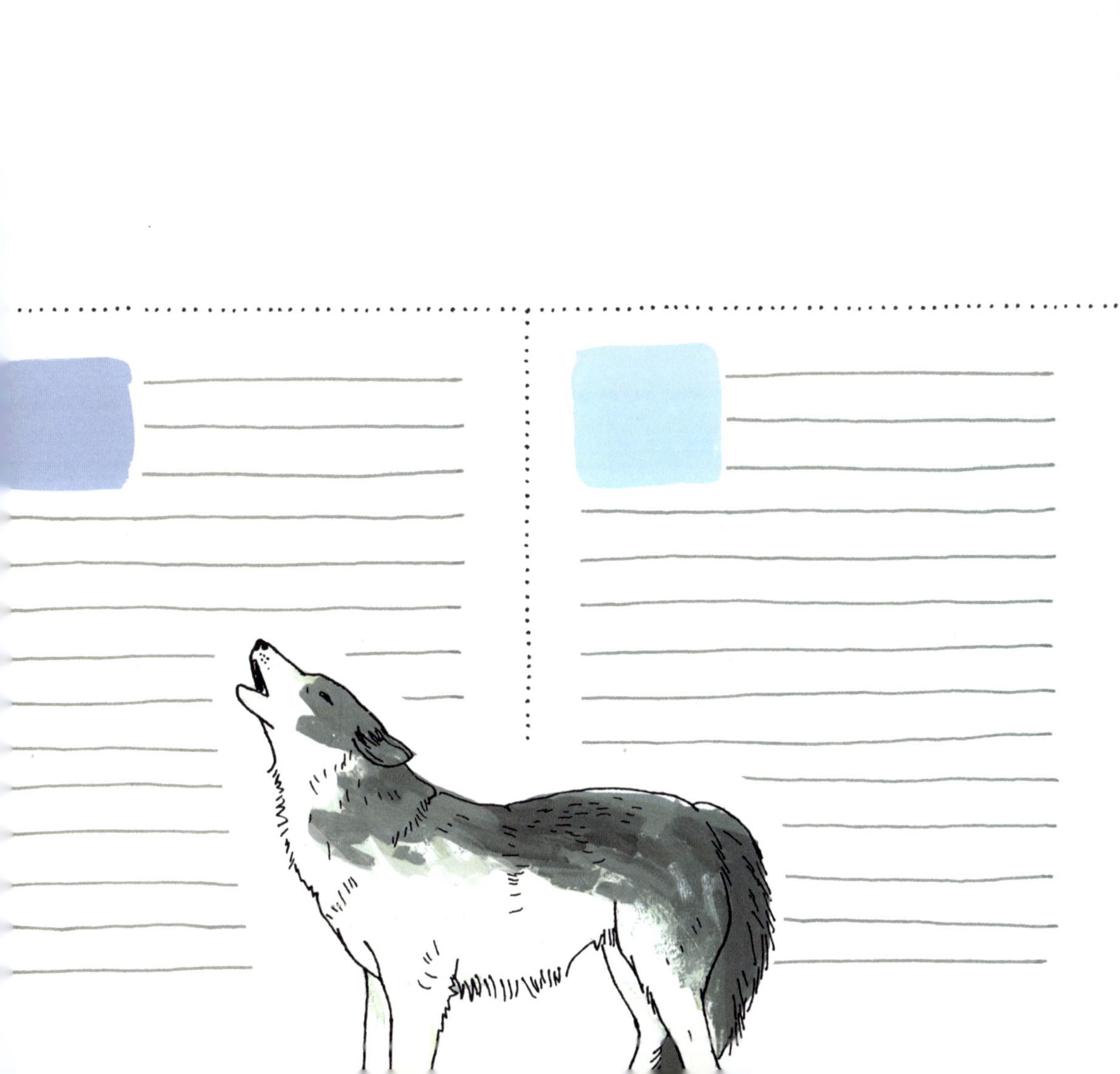

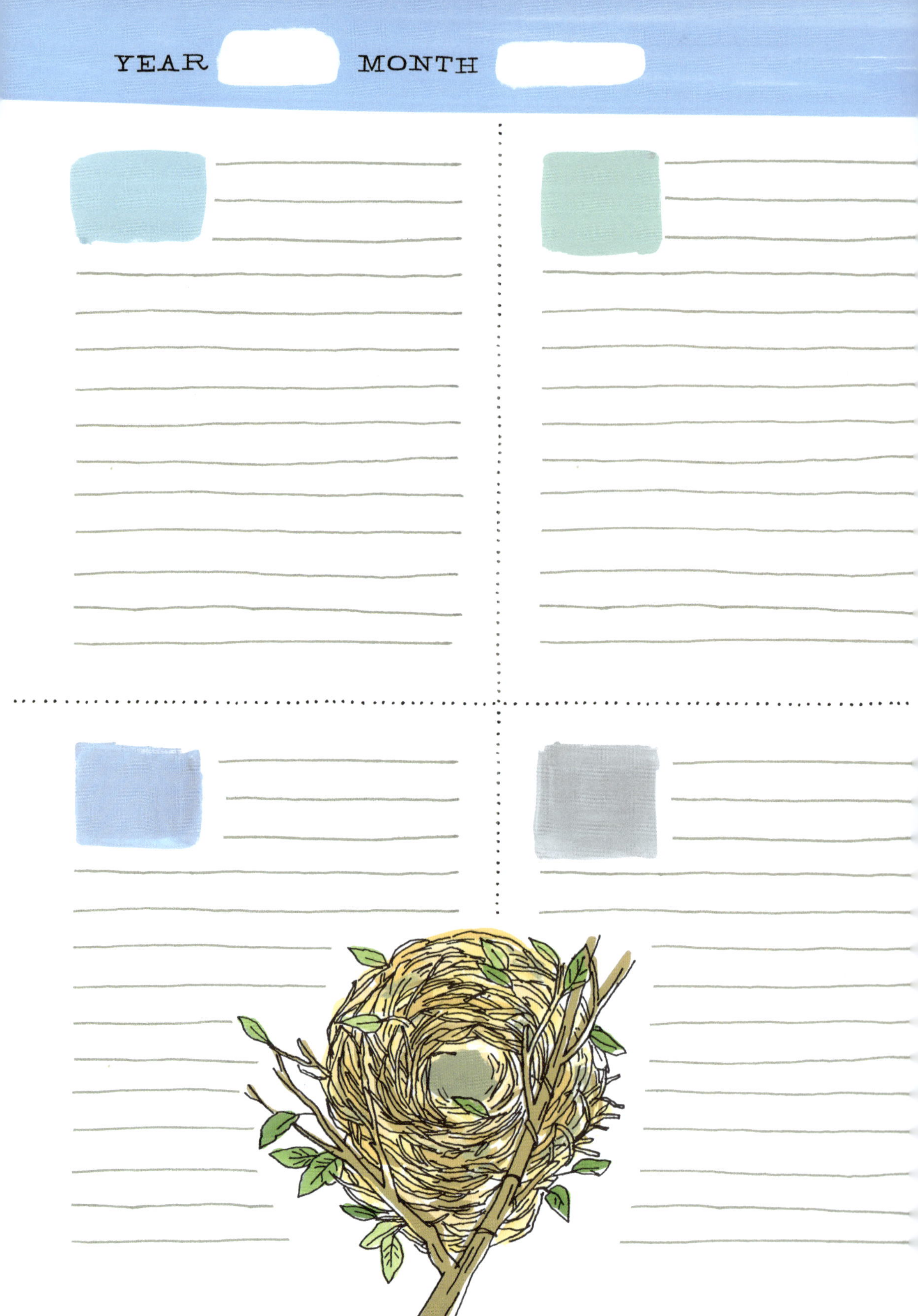

YEAR
MONTH

YEAR
MONTH

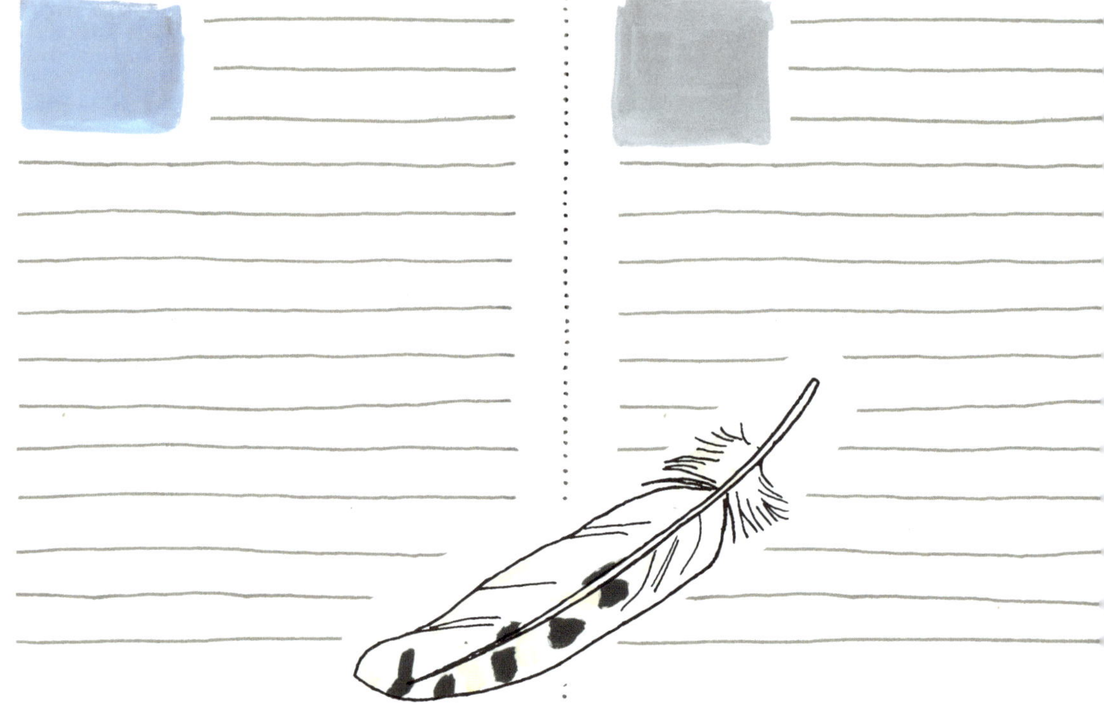

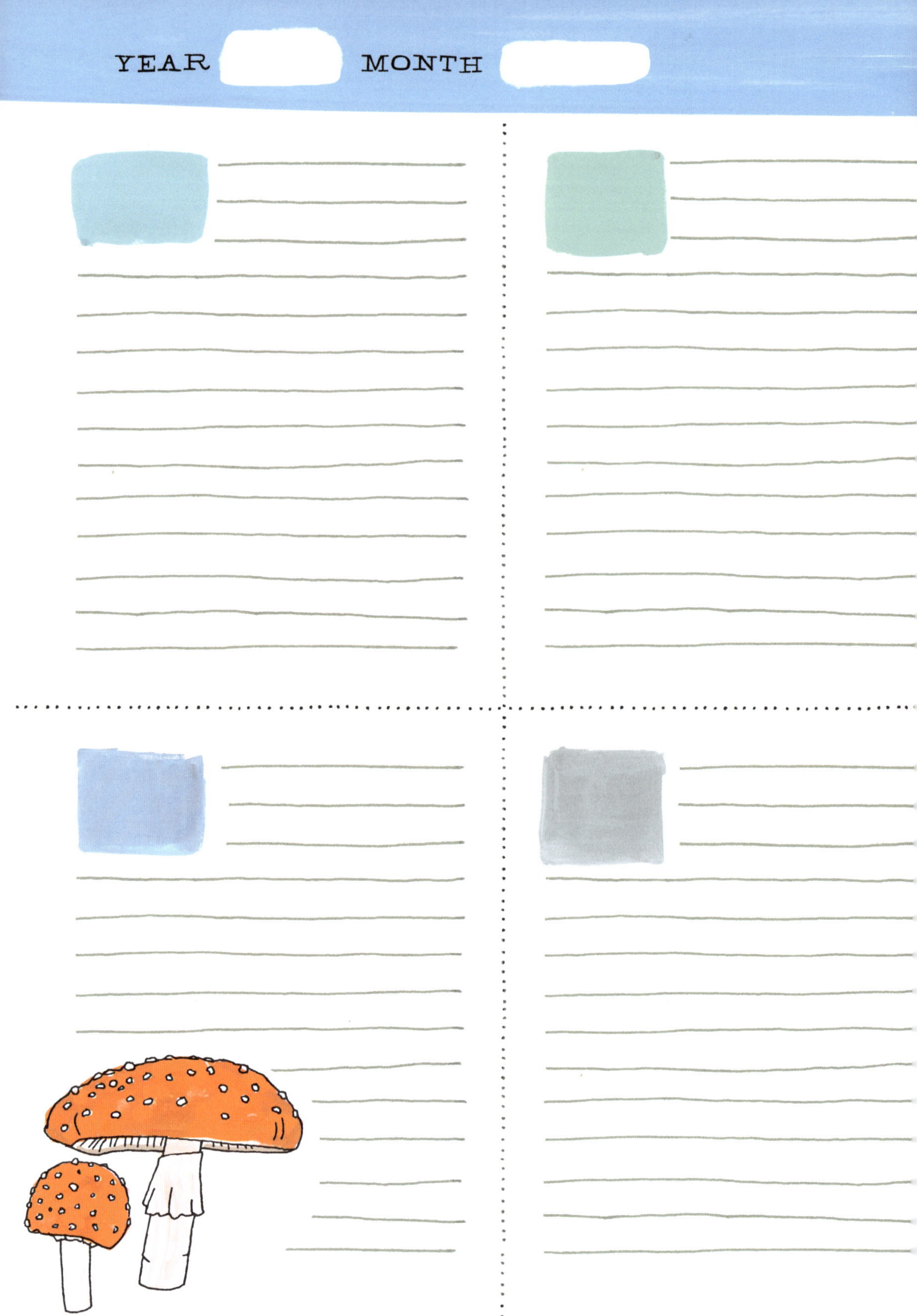

YEAR
MONTH

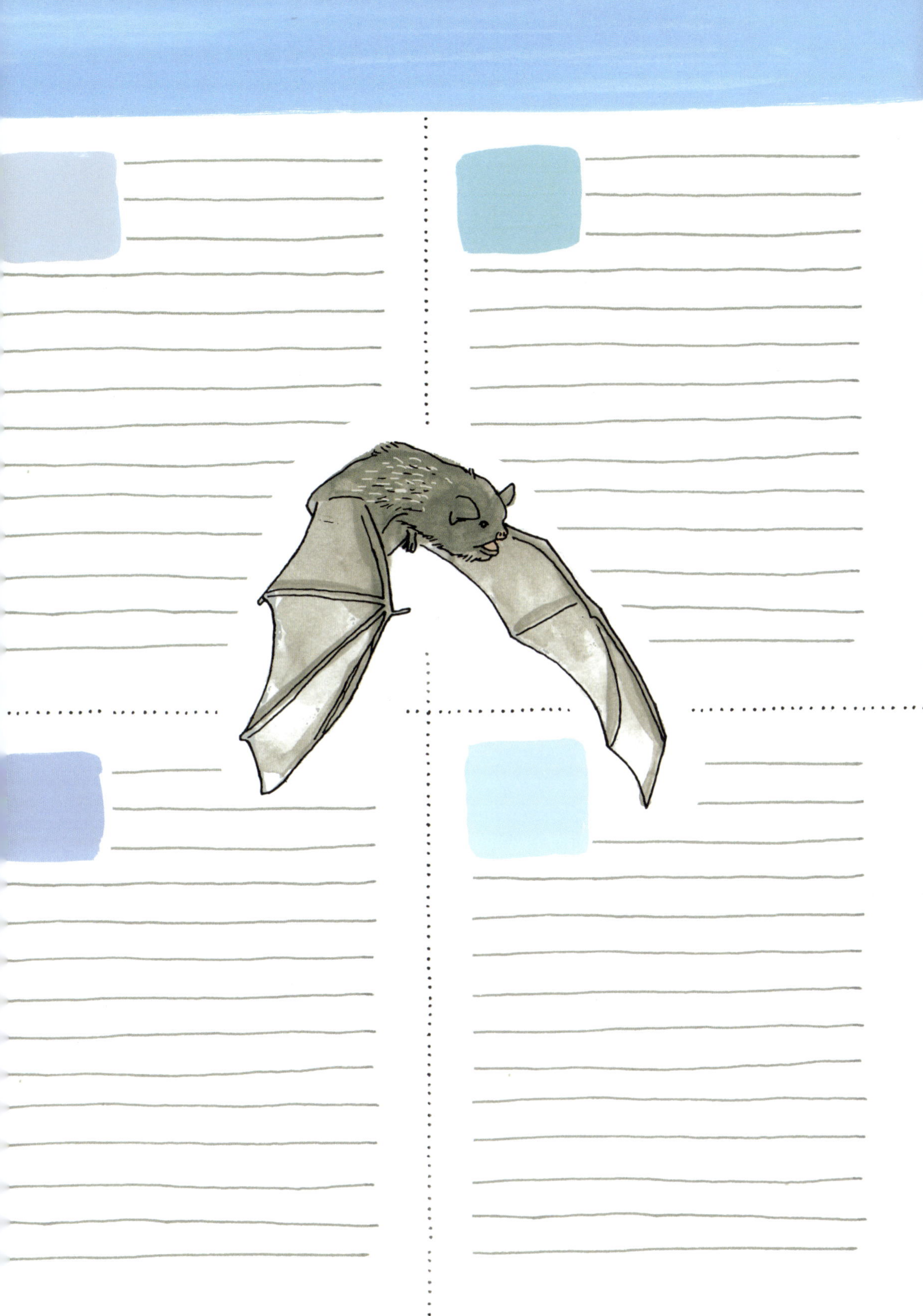

HOW TO DRAW A BAT

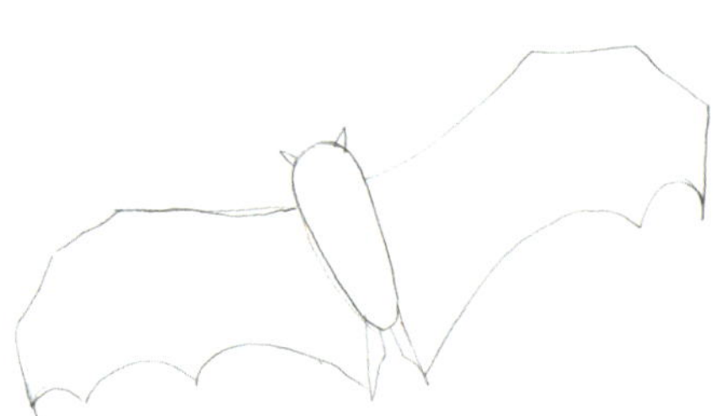

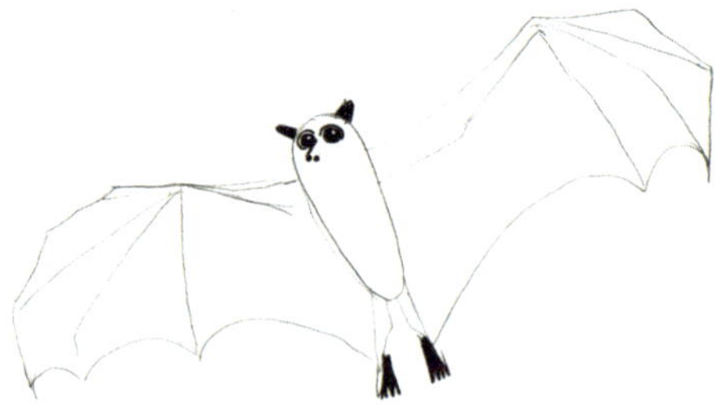

In pencil, sketch the outline of the body including the ears and legs. Sketch the outline of the wings. The width of each wing is about twice the length of the body.

Ink in the eyes, nose, ears, and feet. Sketch lines into the wings that represent five fingers. Look at your own fingers and try to imagine where a bat's knuckles would go.

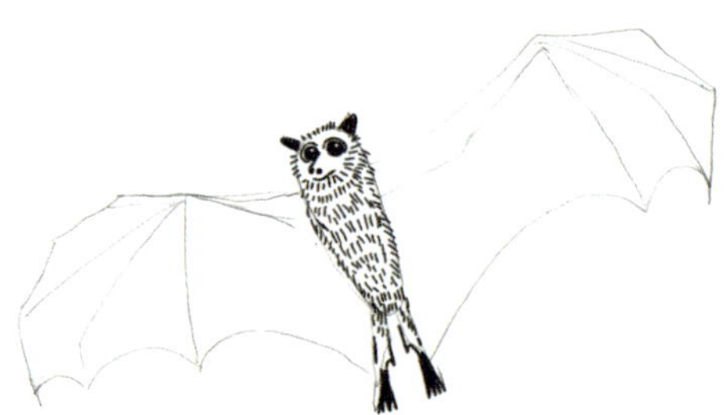

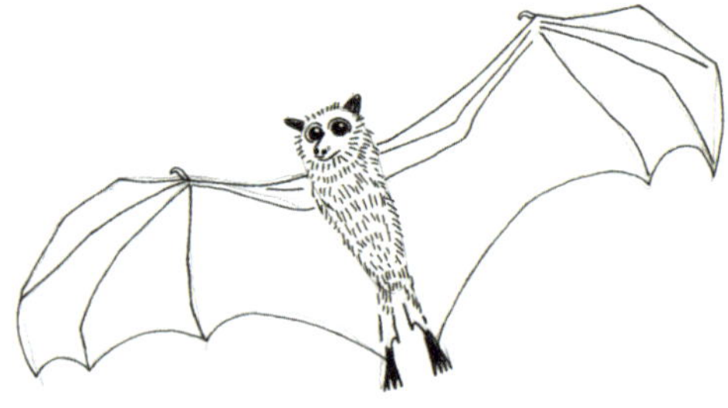

In ink, draw in tiny lines for the fur and add a mouth.

Now trace over the outline of the wings and fingers in ink. Don't forget to add a thumb at the top of each wing!

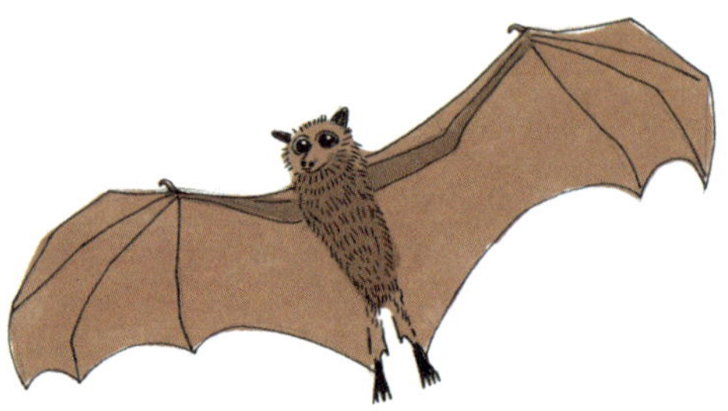

ANATOMY OF A BAT

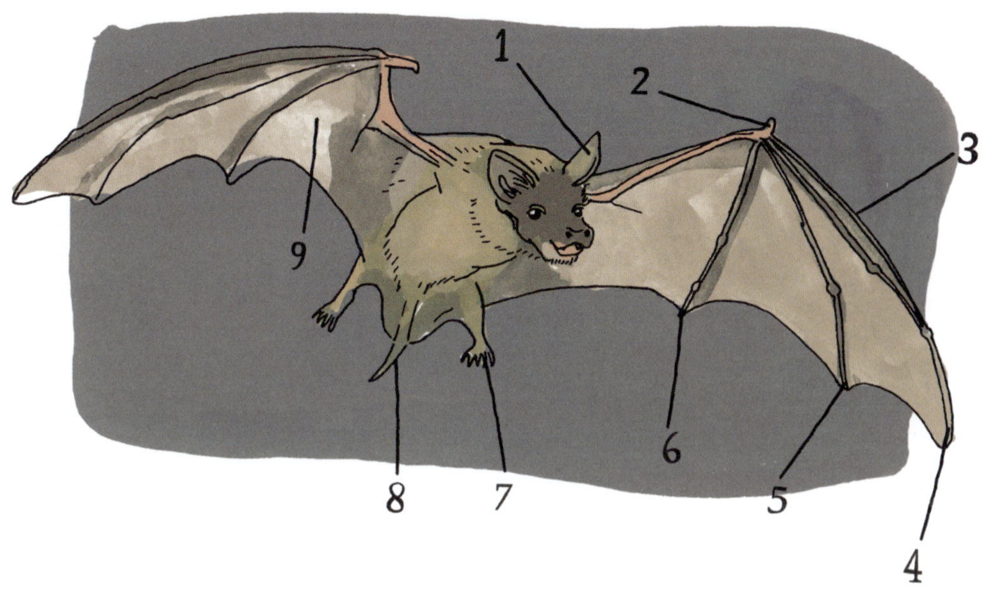

1. ear
2. thumb
3. second finger
4. third finger
5. fourth finger
6. fifth finger
7. foot
8. tail
9. membrane

Bats are the only mammals capable of true flight.

YEAR
MONTH

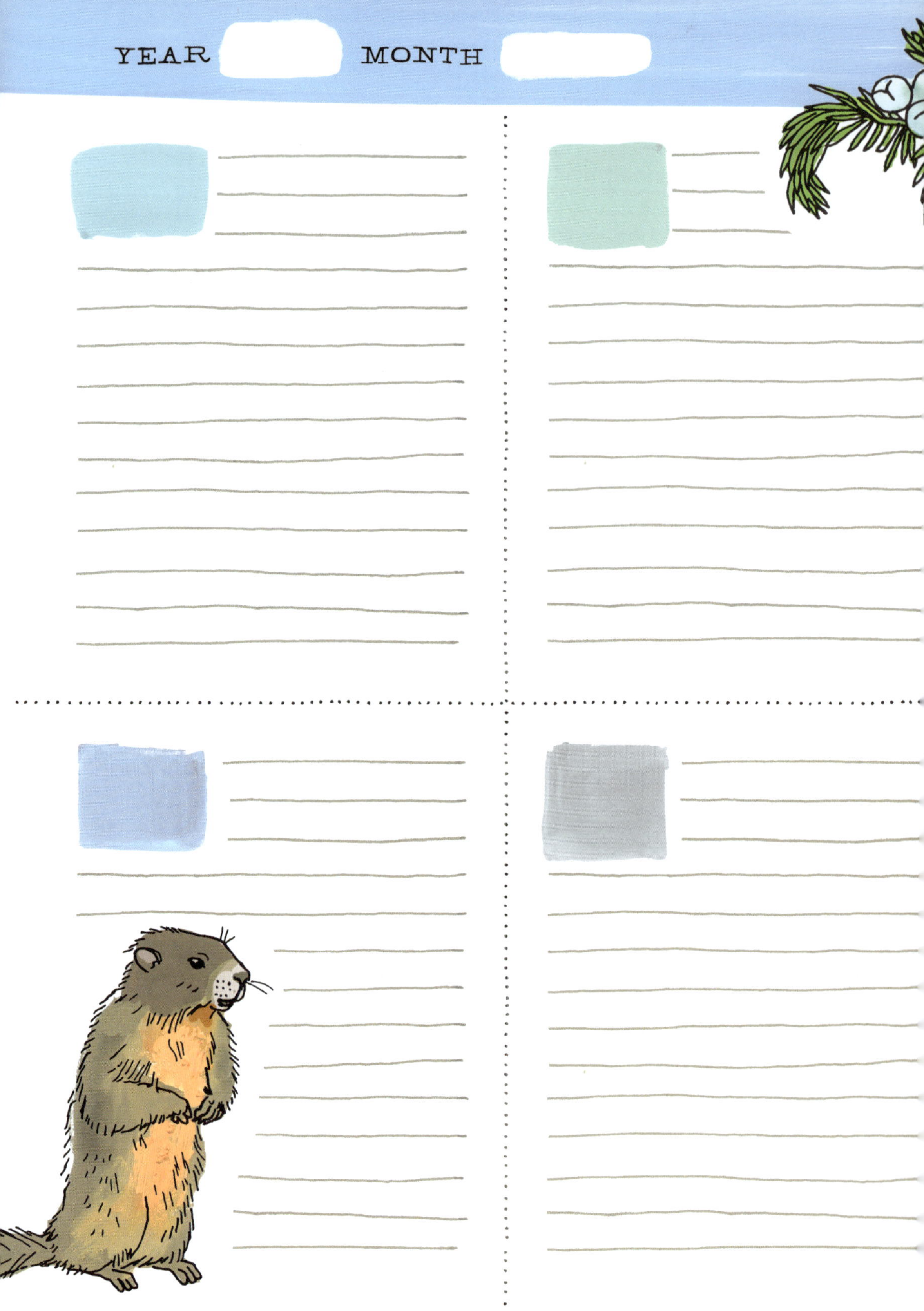

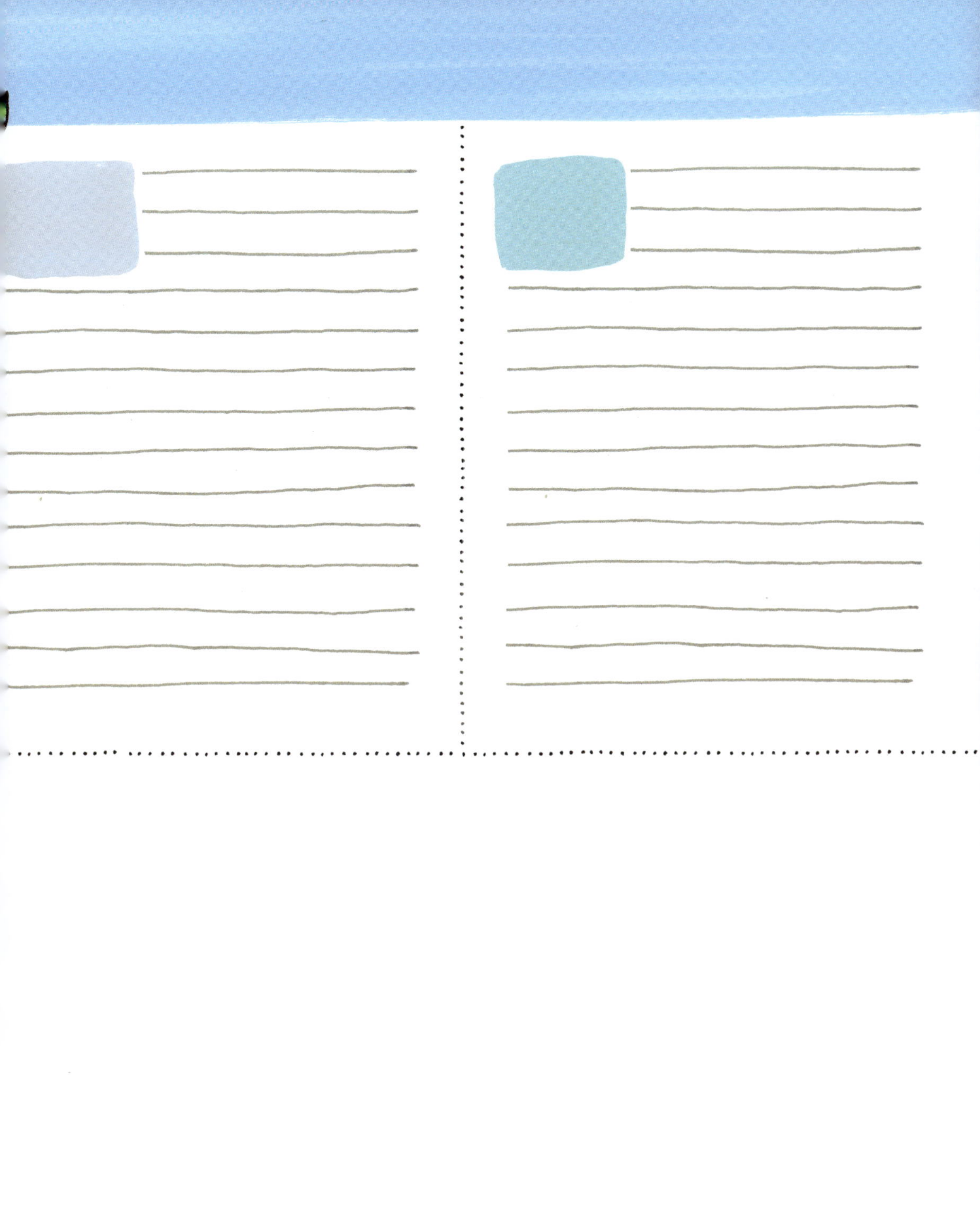

YEAR
MONTH

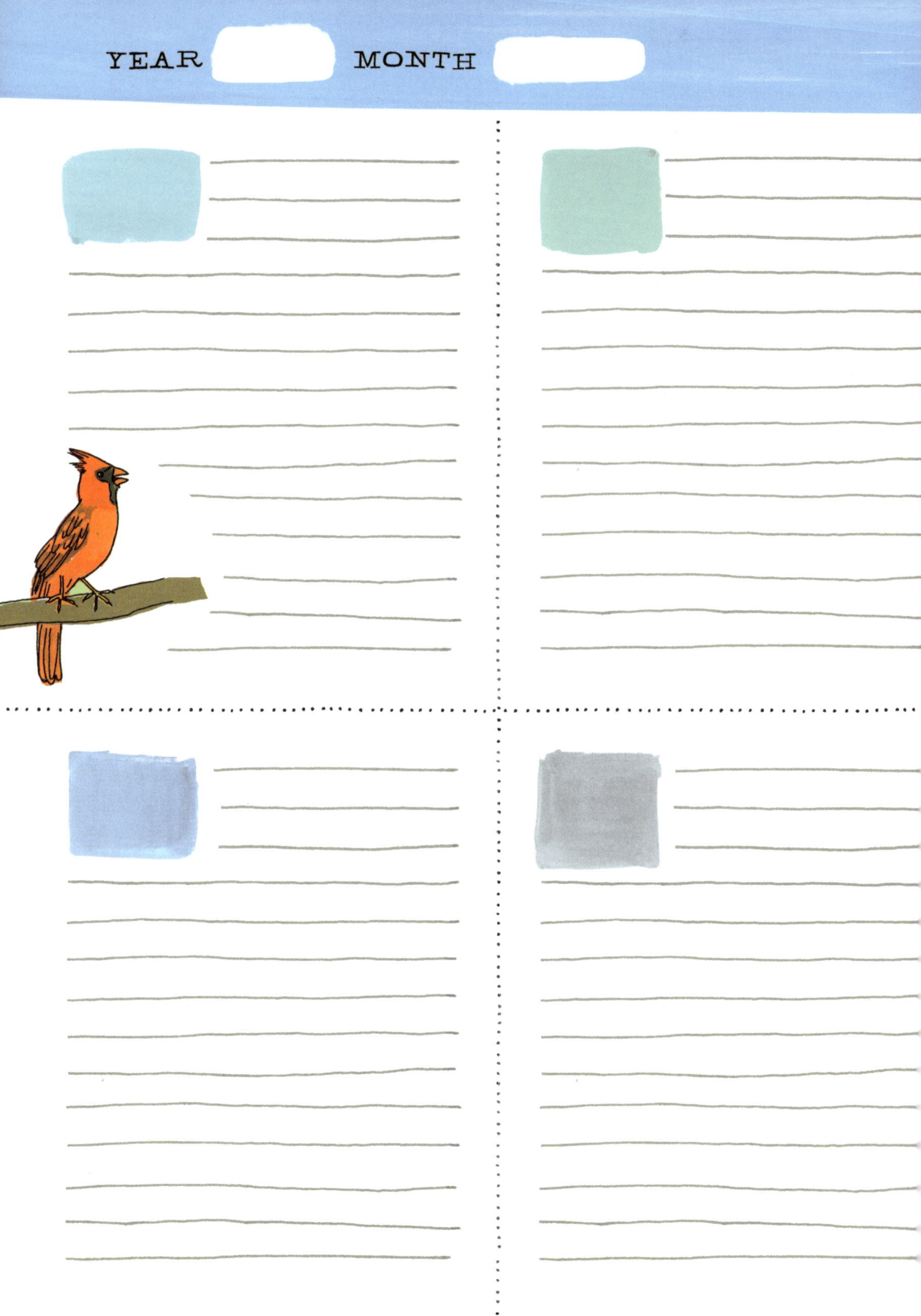

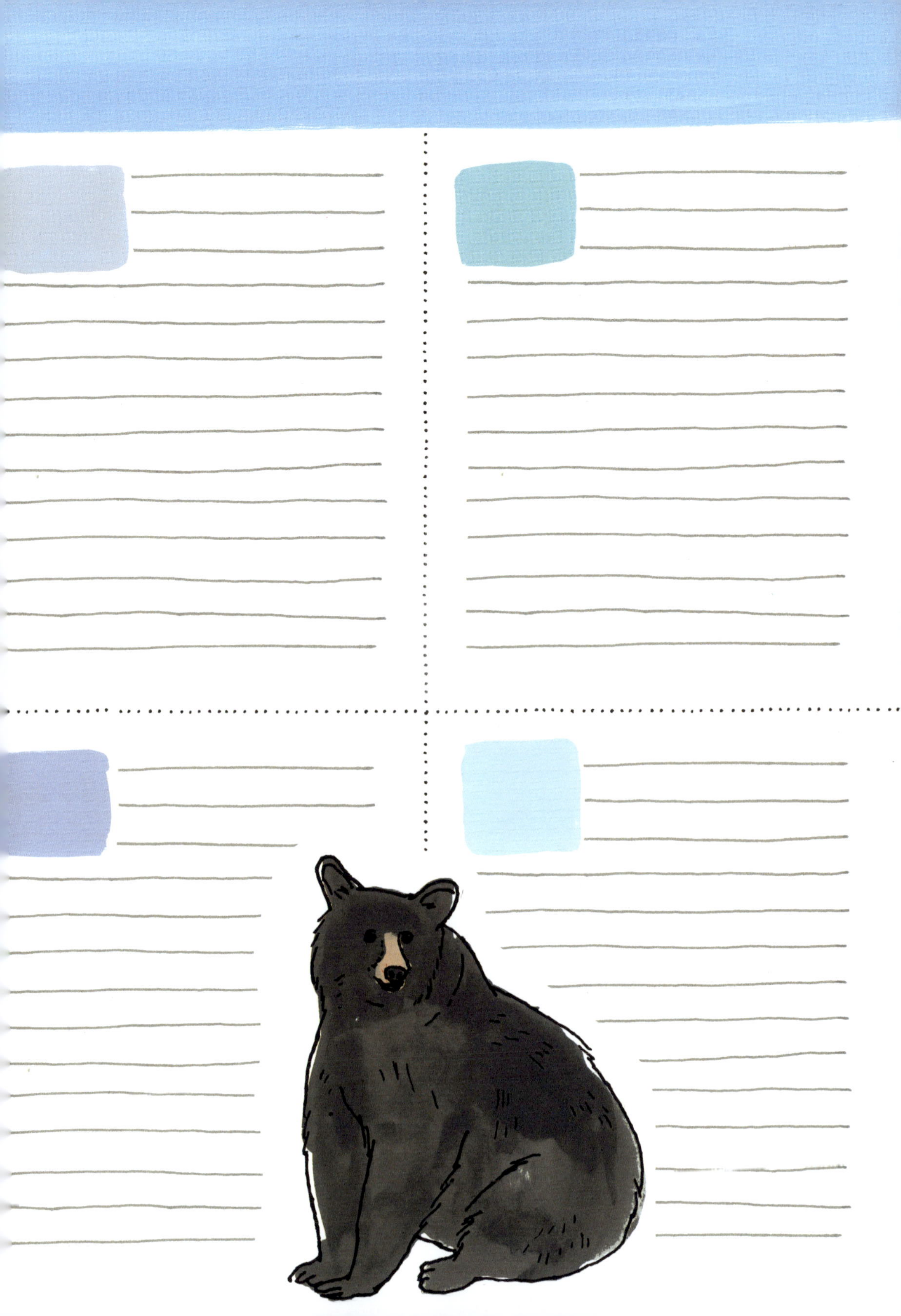

YEAR MONTH

YEAR
MONTH

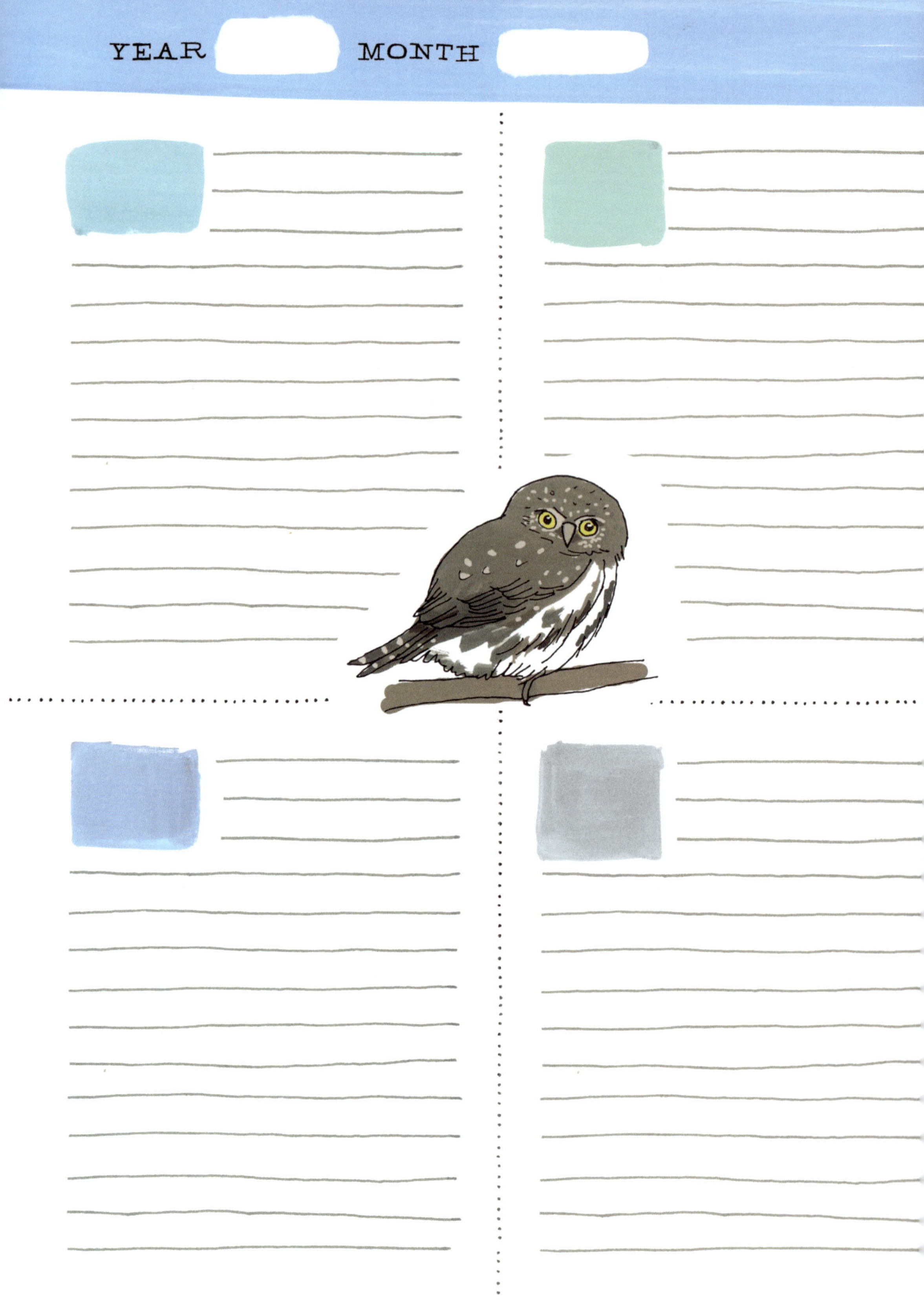

HOW TO DRAW A SNOWFLAKE

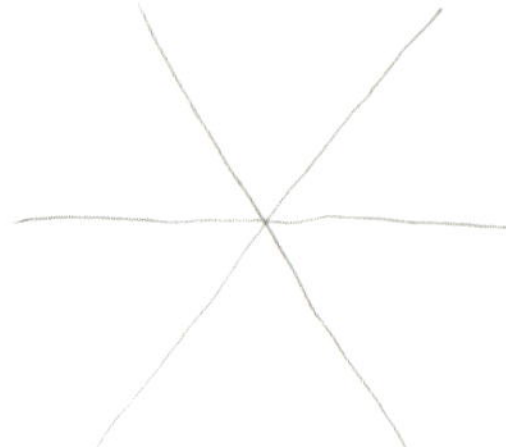

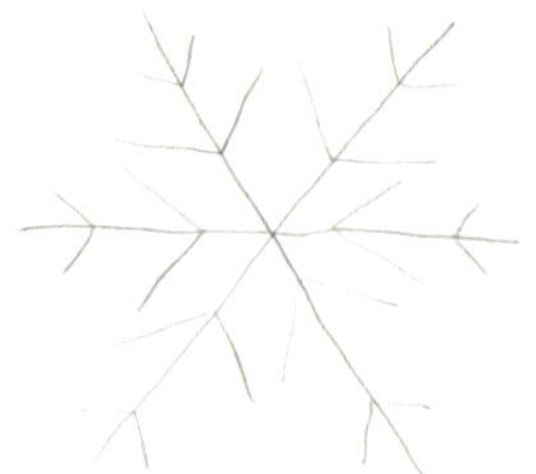

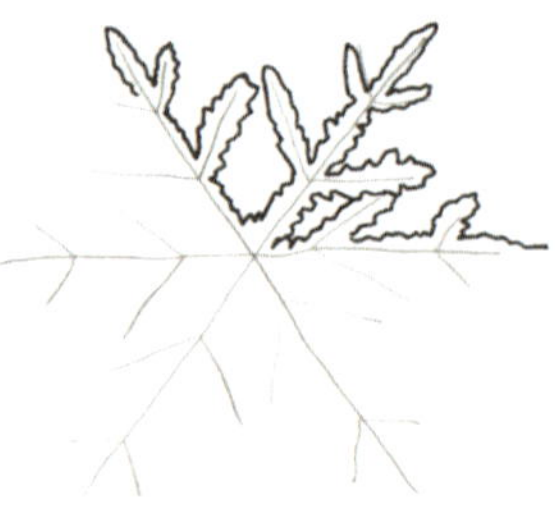

In pencil, sketch an X shape and add a horizontal line through the intersection.

Sketch in small V-shaped lines coming off of each main line.

In ink, begin drawing crystallized ice around each line. Make this outline squiggly to look like the edge of ice.

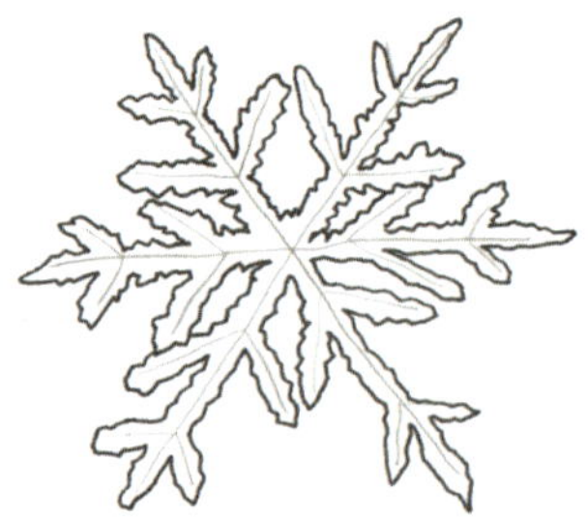

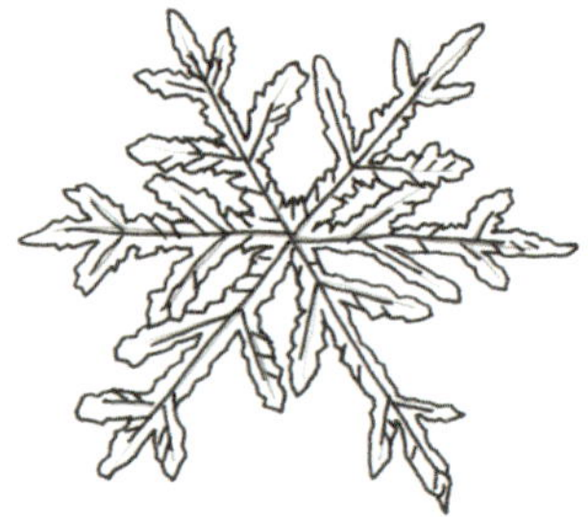

Make your way all the way around each line with this squiggly line until you reach your starting point.

Now go over your original main lines with ink and add other tiny lines here and there for texture.

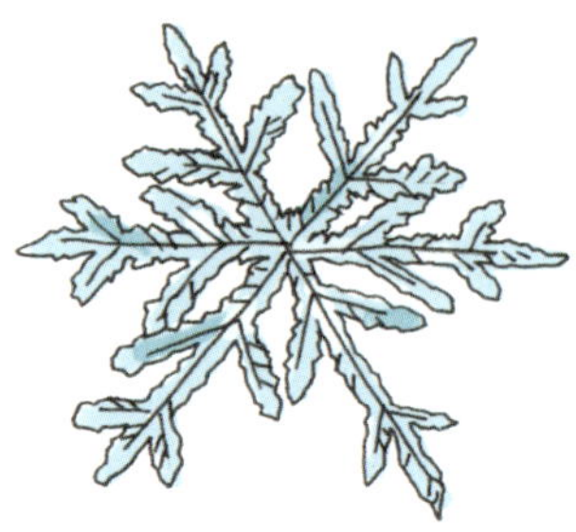

SOME SNOWFLAKE SHAPES

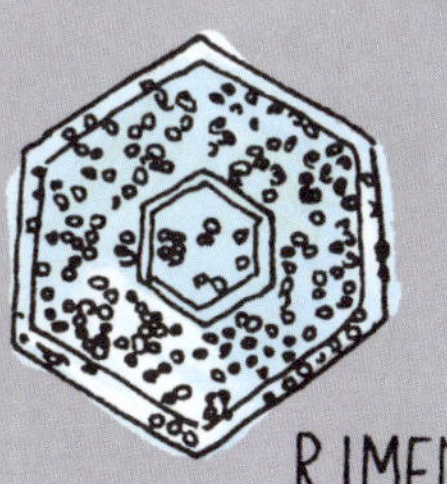

RIMED CRYSTAL

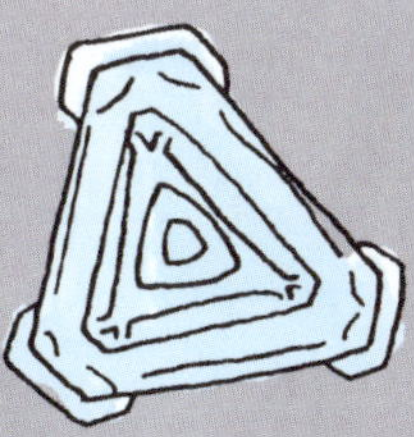

TRIANGULAR FORMS

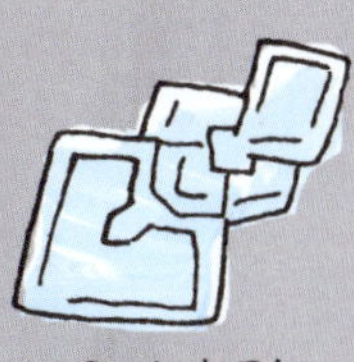

ARROWHEAD

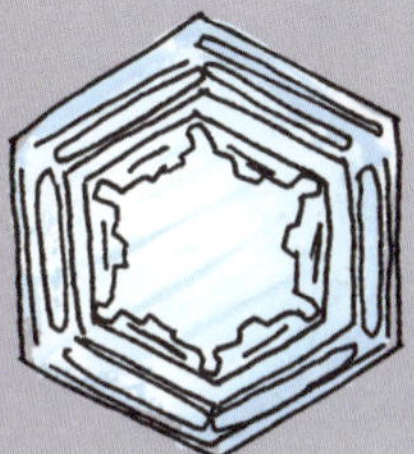

SIMPLE PRISM

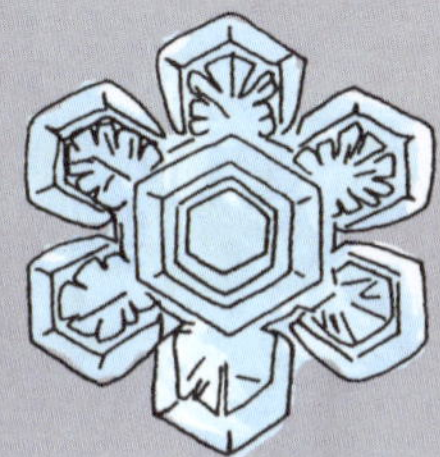

STELLAR PLATE

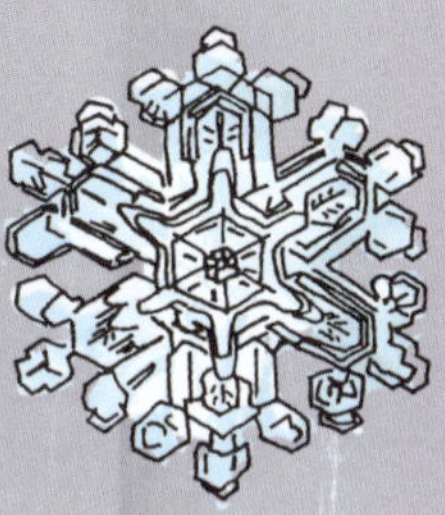

STELLAR DENDRITE

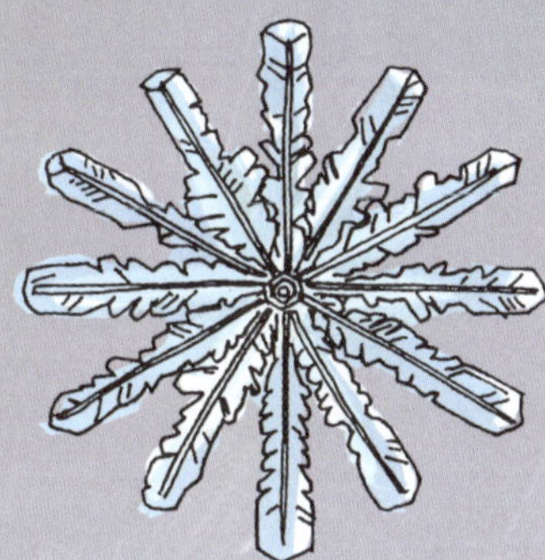

12-SIDED SNOWFLAKE

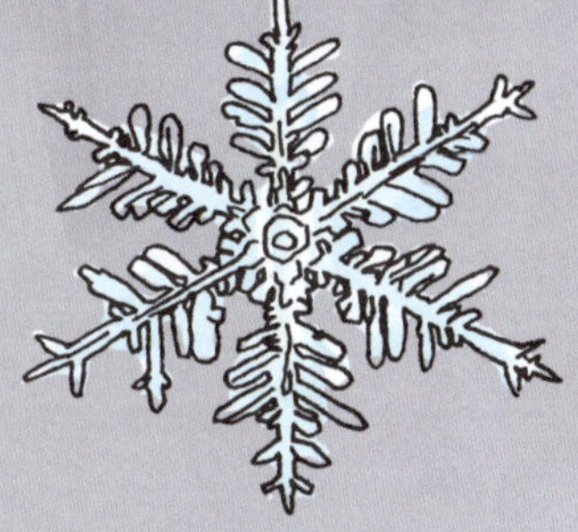

FERNLIKE STELLAR DENDRITE

YEAR   MONTH

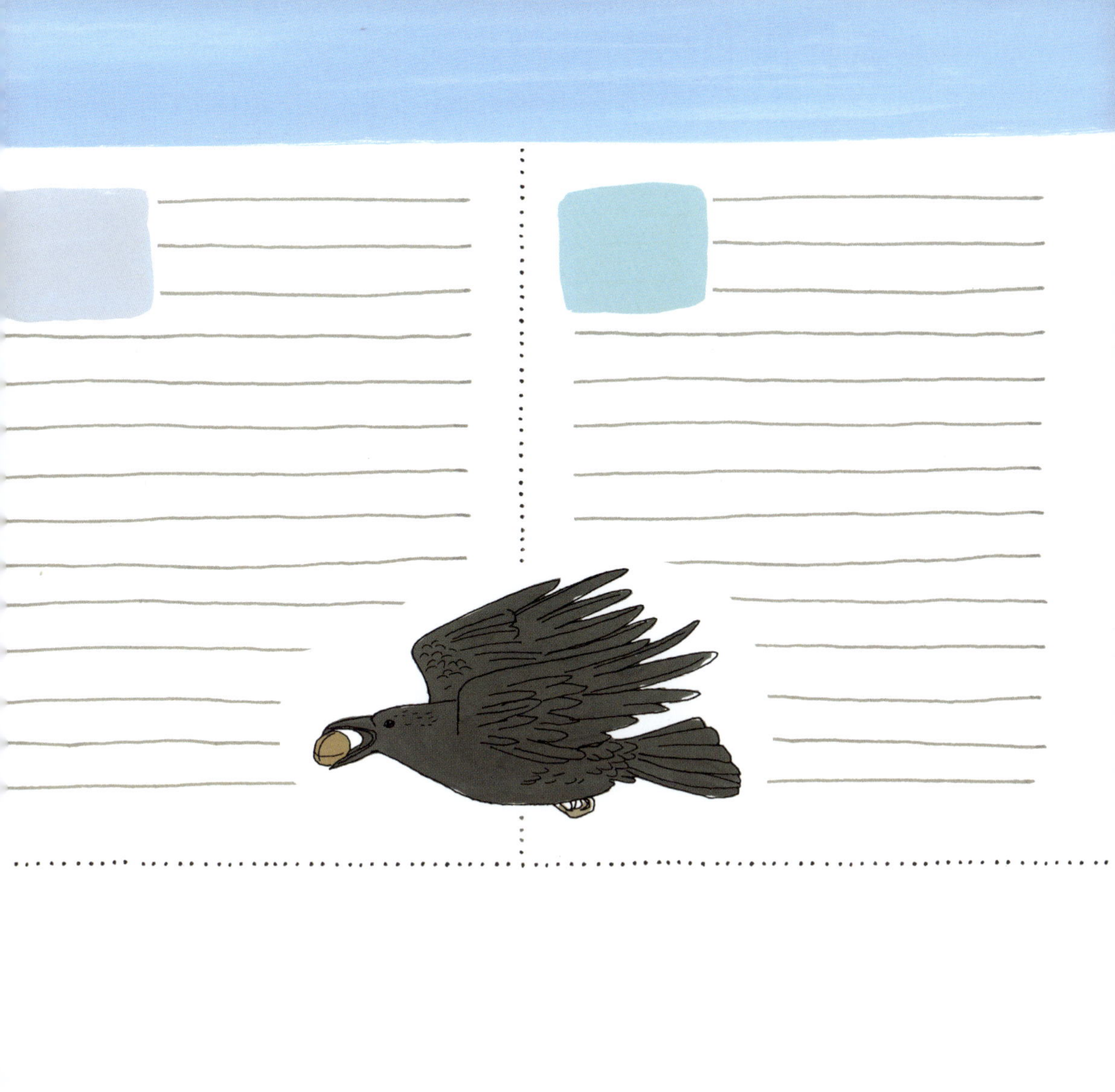

YEAR
MONTH

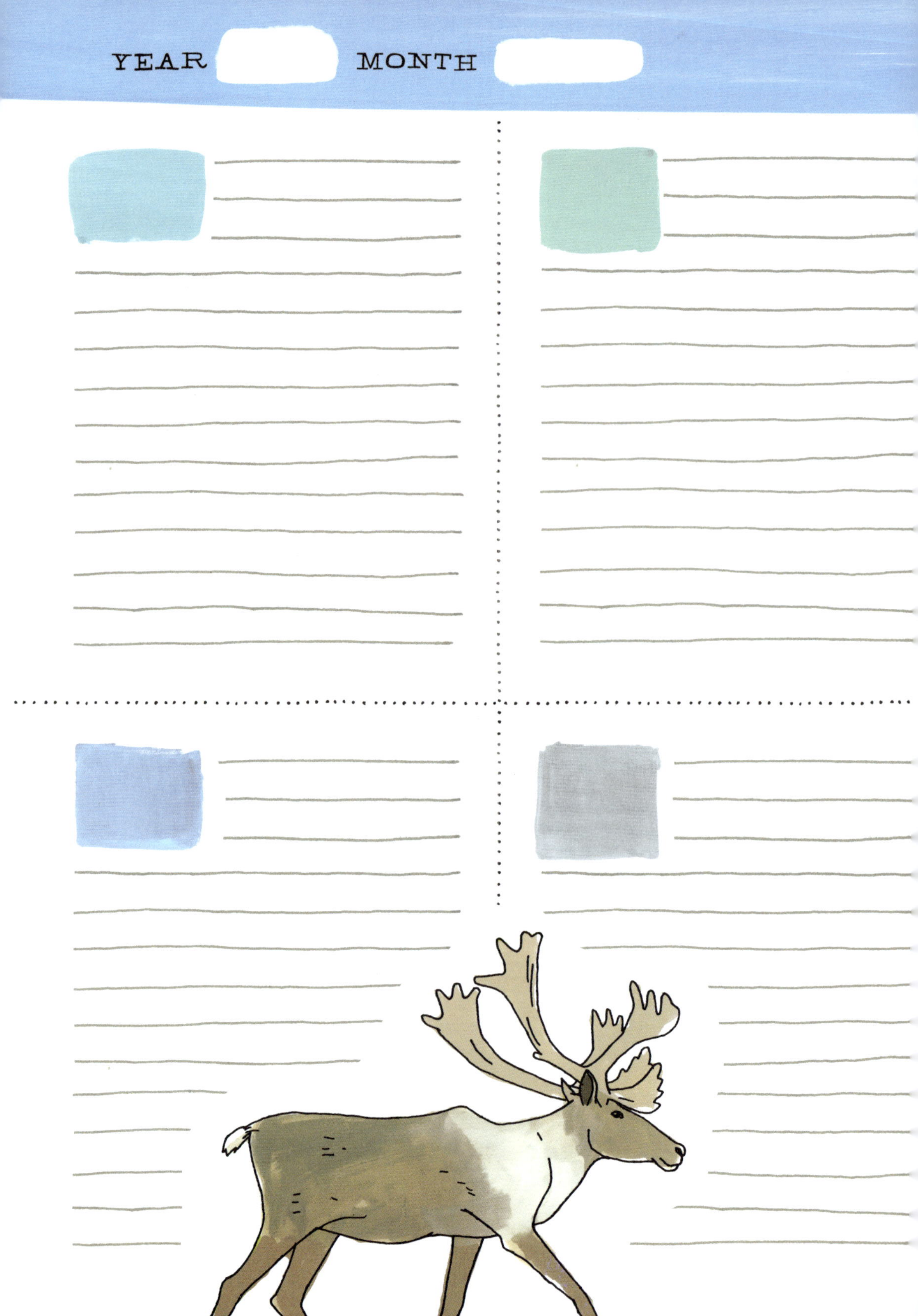

YEAR
MONTH

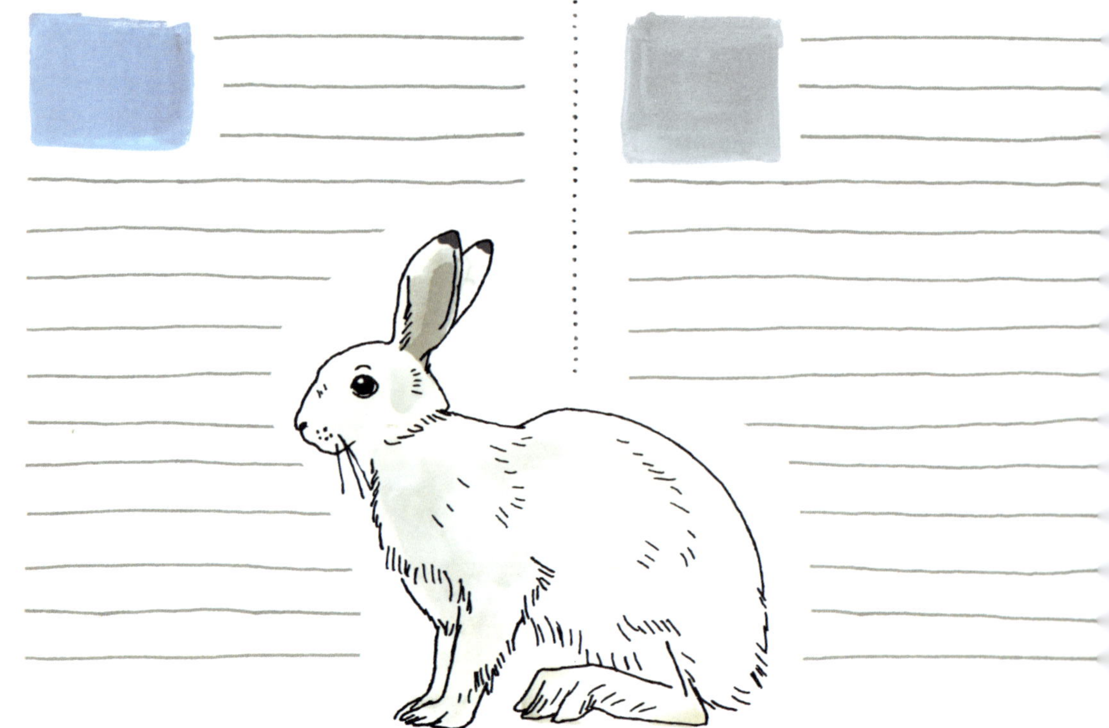

YEAR
MONTH

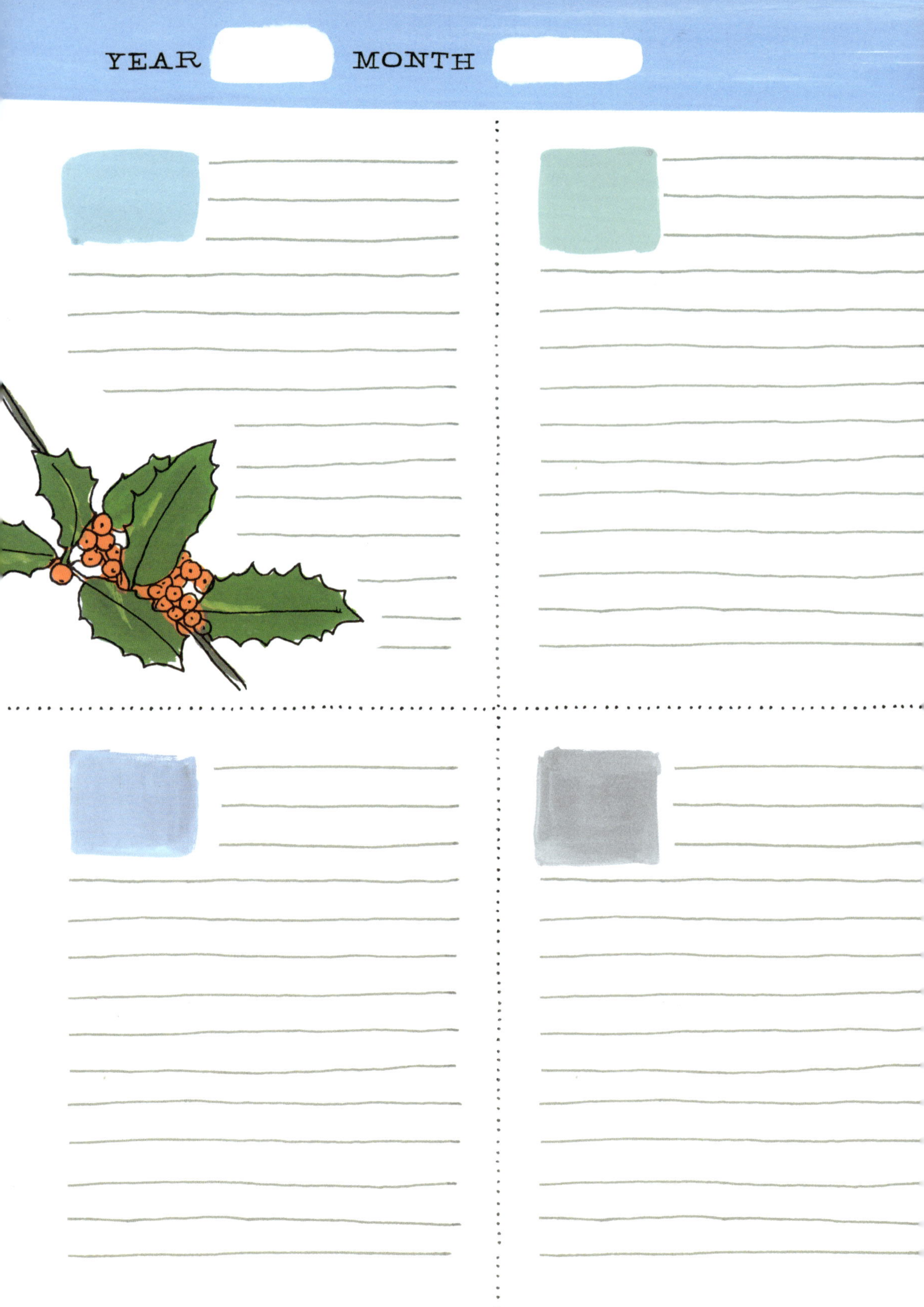

YEAR
MONTH

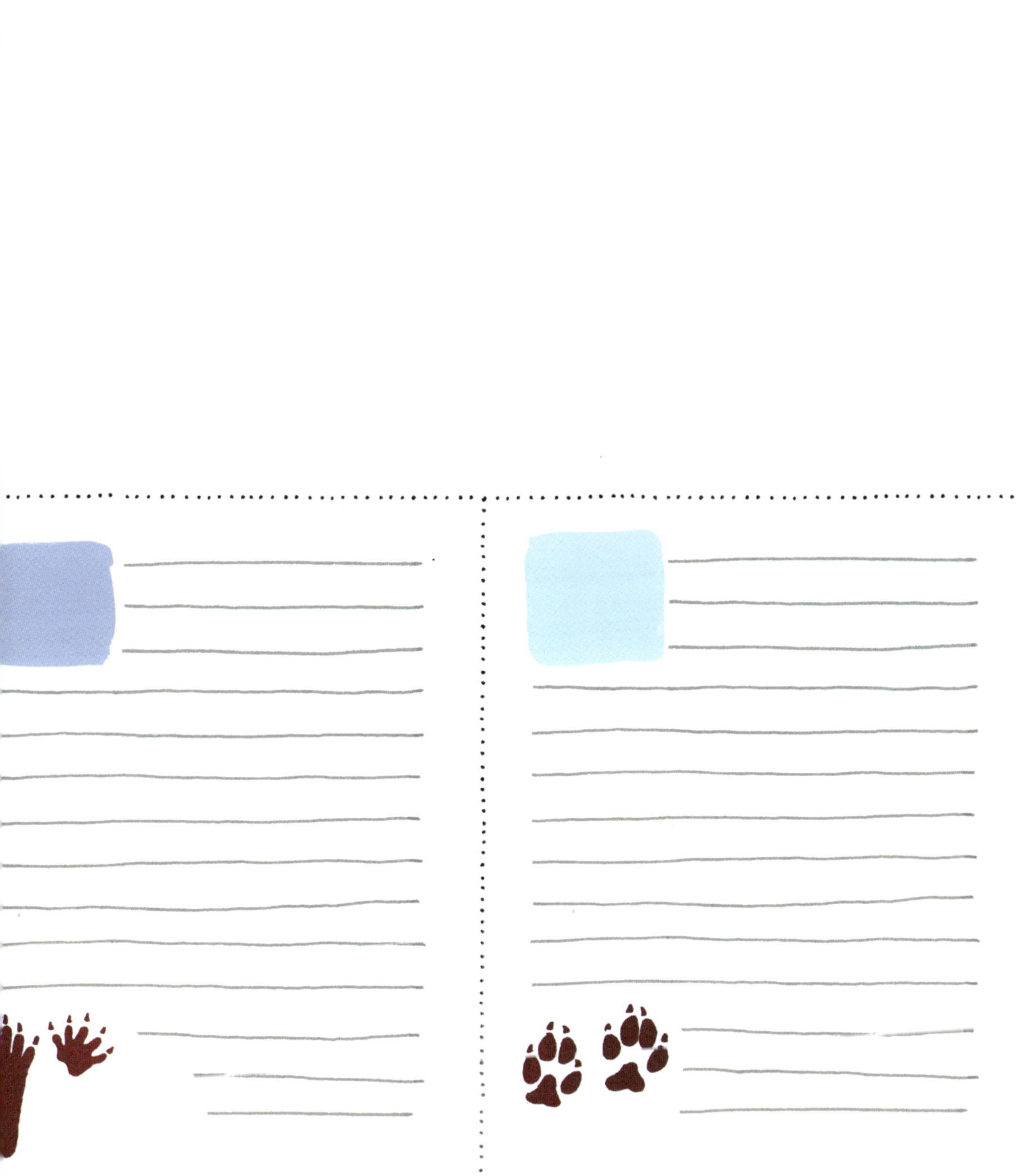

HOW TO DRAW AN ANT

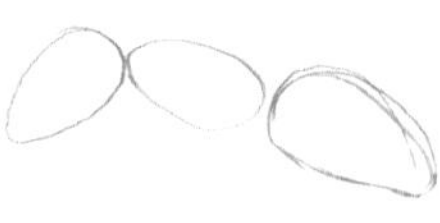

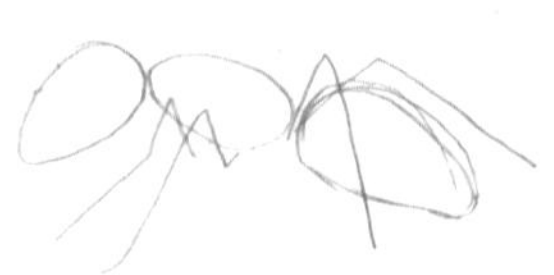

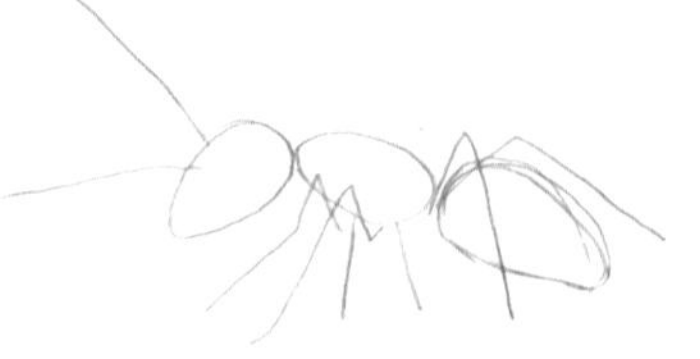

In pencil, sketch three ovals for the head, thorax, and abdomen.

Add four lines with joints in them for legs.

Add two more straight lines for legs on the opposite side of the body, and sketch in the antennae.

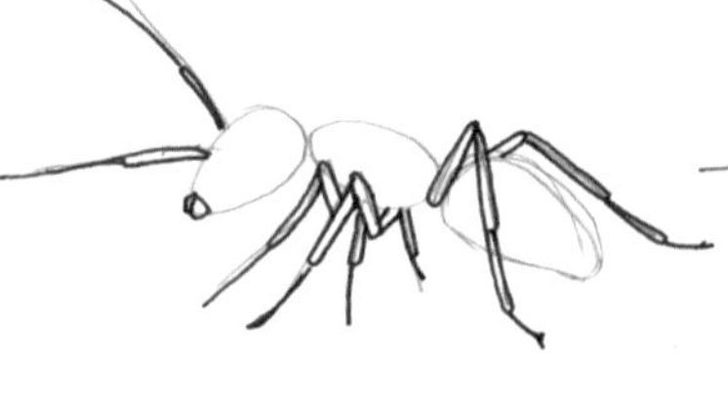

Ink in the legs and antennae. Add the mandibles to the front of the head.

Go over the rest of the body outline in ink.

Add an eye and a few lines to the abdomen for detail.

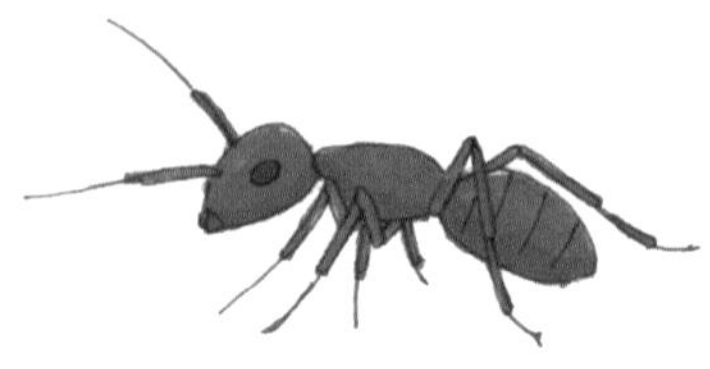

ANATOMY OF AN ANT

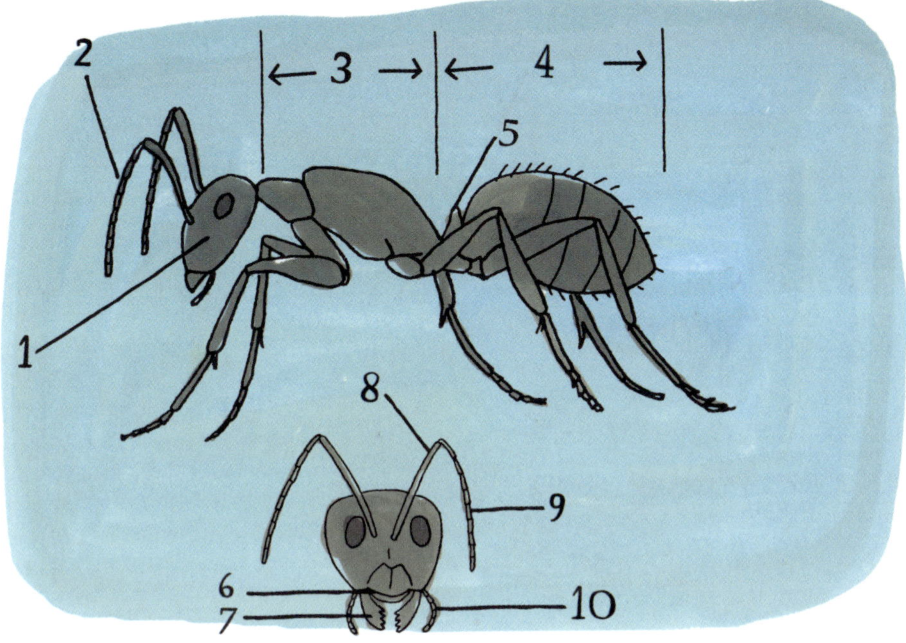

1. **head** - contains the mouth, mandibles, eyes, and antenna
2. **antenna** - used to smell, recognize nest mates, and detect enemies
3. **thorax** - middle region where the three pairs of legs are connected
4. **abdomen or gaster** - contains the vital organs and reproductive parts
5. **petiole** - connects the thorax to the abdomen
6. **labrum** - floor of the mouth
7. **mandible** - used for digging, carrying, collecting food, and building nests
8. **shaft** - base of the antenna
9. **lash** - segmented top of the antenna used for smell
10. **labial palp** - serves the function of a lower lip

Storey Publishing
210 MASS MoCA Way
North Adams, MA 01247
storey.com

Printed in China by R.R. Donnelley
10 9 8 7 6 5 4 3 2